Building
The Information
Asset™

Changing the Face of
Business Intelligence and
Ensuring Your Legacy

Decision Intelligence Model ™
—————————————————— *
Data Flow Architecture Foundation

Joseph Kokinda

ISBN 0-7414-4223-X

Published by:

INFI∞ITY
PUBLISHING.COM

1094 New DeHaven Street, Suite 100
West Conshohocken, PA 19428-2713
Info@buybooksontheweb.com
www.buybooksontheweb.com
Toll-free (877) BUY BOOK
Local Phone (610) 941-9999
Fax (610) 941-9959

Printed in the United States of America

Printed on Recycled Paper

Published December 2007

To Georgette and Joey
For all of your love and continuous support...

Table of Contents

Section III – The Legacy

Introduction

The scene is a large boardroom. Managers have just arrived from across the organization for this very important meeting. Today our company will decide whether or not to sell one of its facilities and merge with a leading competitor. The information used to make this decision needs to be accurate and up-to-the-minute. Unfortunately, the managers have arrived with only the best data they could get their hands on prior to the meeting. They show up with information from a number of different sources in a variety of formats with inconsistent freshness. HR data has come from an Access database built and maintained by HR. Customer information has been assembled in an Excel-based scorecard, which is built and managed by a consultant working for one of the business units. Finance numbers are on printed reports from the financial applications system. Budget and forecast data are cut and pasted from an Excel application and printed for reference. There is also marketing data used, which is assembled from Internet sources. On top of all that, other data exists in someone's head from a conversation they just had on the phone and is spread by word of mouth. With all of this, the meeting starts...

As the discussion ensues, it becomes apparent there are issues. "Well, my reports say this and your reports say that." "Your numbers are 1, 2, 3? Well, those numbers don't match my numbers." At this rate, it appears the company will be making a best guess as to what to do. What will be the decision? Will it be the right decision? Is there any reason, given the technology we have today, that organizational management should be going through this type of chaos when trying to make basic but critical business decisions? I don't think so — at least no good reason.

Unfortunately, this scene is commonplace in many organizations today. This is how decisions are being made. Right or wrong, there's no need for this anymore. The investments on IT over the past thirty years have created all the pieces required to put together the first true information management and delivery system. This complete architecture and delivery system is The Information Asset™.

In the following chapters, I will walk you through the discussions on our way to completely changing how organizations operate by enabling the hidden and invaluable asset that exists or can exist in every company today. This is The Information Asset™.

In Section I, we'll discuss important background to provide some motivation and historical insights in the following chapters:

[Motivation]   → Chapter I   Making the Case
[History]   → Chapter II   The Stage is Set

With that background, we'll move into Section II and get into the details of understanding the Information Asset and all of its components. We'll then outline an approach or recipe to assist with the challenging task of making this happen in the "real world." These steps will be covered in the following chapters:

[Definition]   → Chapter III   The Information Asset

[Architecture] → Chapter IV   The Foundation:
                                    Data   Flow   Architecture
                                    Components

[Solution Delivery] →Chapter V Solution Delivery and Management

[The Recipe]   →Chapter VI   "The Recipe"
                                   Building The Information Asset

And finally, in Section III, once we've laid down where we're going and how to get there, our final discussion point will be how to measure success and integrate with future direction. This will be covered in the following chapter:

[The Legacy]   →Chapter VII   Ensuring Your Legacy

Through these three sections and seven chapters, we will travel a long way from the problems and major issues that exist within information technology today to the opportunities and direction that can be taken to resolve these situations. Every tomorrow will look like today unless we take steps to

2

enable and enact effective change. Only through quality work today can we build a better tomorrow.

As discussed in the opening example, it's a wonder that business can operate with the approach that has been taken in reference to organizational data and information. For years, "reporting" has been one of these "we know we need it, but don't want to spend money on it" areas. As much as that made sense for years, data warehousing, data marts, portals, and business intelligence have recently been able to drive some real tangible value to the table. Businesses that make strides in these areas have made great progress in increasing their value, growth and success in the marketplace.

Just consider how important having good information or reporting is in the real world today. Should our country attack another country because they have nuclear weapons? Should we recall all of our medical products because someone died from taking one of our aspirin? Do we evacuate a city before a hurricane hits that will cause major loss of life? Do you execute a person for a crime? Do you operate on someone's heart because they felt a chest pain? Big decisions like these occur every day in the world. For each of these, the people making the decisions require valid and accurate information, knowledge, and decision intelligence to choose the best approach. With the best information, the best choices will be made. With less than the best, poor decisions will be made.

Well, the same applies to business. Big decisions occur every day in every company. Each decision requires information, knowledge and intelligence to support it. Who are our best customers? Should we acquire this other company or build ourselves? Where do we open a new store? How do we market our services? What skills do our people have? How many people work here? What's our current pipeline of opportunities for expansion? These are all interesting questions that could be answered in the most effective ways if the people making decisions had the decision intelligence information they needed when they needed it.

With the value of organizational data and information more apparent than it's ever been in the past, over the next few years the people in the roles of the CIO, CKO, and Technology Management will find themselves in the spotlight. It's not the operational "Wahh, my PC is broken!" spotlight, but rather the "Information and Intelligence" spotlight. Businesses can no longer afford to sit back and approach information delivery and reporting as an area where each department does its own thing and people manually reconcile their reporting or business intelligence during decision-making timeframes. There are huge inefficiencies and poor-quality results from this process and the fragmented technology solutions that support this approach.

Let's pretend that your job running a team, department, or business is like driving a car. Businesses, like cars, move from Point A to Point B while achieving objectives. Along the way, both businesses and cars need to make sure they comply with laws, don't run out of gas, and don't crash, etc. Also, businesses and cars both need information and resources to be successful, and need to speed up or slow down based upon road conditions or weather. Sound like a fair analogy? To make the point, there are a number of great similarities.

So, if your team, department, or organization is your car, then let's put you in the driver's seat. Since you're driving, you are responsible for everyone in the car. With the way management is expected to run businesses today, we'll just need to make one change. To make the analogy more consistent, you would be driving the car — but without the dashboard, which shows you the information you need. Just as in most companies today, management is expected to make decisions and be responsible for people, but these resources are not given the informational solutions they need to do the best job possible. They usually have to assemble and gather this information while en route at 80 mph.

Now, this is where it gets interesting. Since, in business, you think you know how solve these problems without good information or intelligence, you pretend you don't need a dashboard or detailed information and move on. You're content "flying blind" because "Hey, everyone else is." In other words, you just accept it. What might happen if you just accepted this in your car?

Let's take your car on the highway. Without a dashboard, let's attempt to apply business "lack-of-information" techniques to resolve our missing dashboard:

- **How fast am I going? I don't want to get a ticket...**
  To solve this, with your corresponding business experience, you hire a team of consultants to drive with you in the car. Some employees tell you how fast you're going every time you ask. But you don't believe them and you think the

consultants know better. The methods the consultants employ include telling you what you already know or making very general estimates. (And so goes the old joke of hiring consultants. They steal your watch and then tell you the time.) In any case, you need to keep asking people how fast you're going all along the way.

- **How much fuel do I have? Should I stop to get gas?**
  Well, since you're driving and have no gas gauge, you'll need to hire someone to figure this out. They will need to climb out on the moving car upon request and stick a dipstick into the gas tank. Safe to say, this will get challenging when you start running low on fuel and need to find a fueling station. The Chief Fuel Officer also then hires some other employees to assist in gathering this information and providing you with historical trends and forecasts, etc…

- **Time and Temperature**
  You know, you just don't have room or need experts in this area. Good request to outsource. You say you'll just call someone for time and outside temperature updates. When you actually try using this method, you realize people on the other side of the world are telling you it's sunny, when it's raining outside. Not looking so good.

- **Check Oil**
  Same problem as gas, but you'll need to stop to get a reading on this. You have no Check Oil alert to warn of a problem. You don't want to run out of oil. Your car just might blow up under these circumstances. You hire someone to manage this. Well, now the person you hired tells you we need to stop every 100 miles so he can get out and check the oil. How can you keep stopping for this when the competition doesn't need to stop? How can you beat your competitors to Point B when you keep having to stop and check the oil?

- **Check Engine**
  No Check Engine light — oh, great. If your car has a problem, it's just going to stop working with no warning. You decide maybe you'll need to reinvest in a redundant system — you know, another car that just sits and waits for the existing car to break. Hmmm . . . not very cost effective, but probably worthwhile.

- **Rules and Regulations?**

Need resources for this, too. Wow, the car is getting full, but you need someone to advise on local laws and regulations. Not sure if your blinkers are working, or if your emissions are correct, or how to speak with an officer of the law if pulled over. You don't want to be pulled over for violations because you've got a full carload of people to take care of.

- **Navigation**
  At this point, the car is full and it looks like we'll need more space to carry all the people. Maybe we should upgrade to an SUV or bus. Not sure. Well, what about trying to get where we're going? With all these people, everyone's hiring their own people with GPS tracking and maps and methods for telling you how to get to Point B. There's major redundancy, but hey, things are already out of control. Also, it's starting to smell a little funky in the back seat. Anyone bring a tree air freshener?

Well, I think you get the picture. Oh, how simple, yet important, the concept of a having a dashboard or effective access to information is. Driving your car and taking a long trip without your auto dashboard would be major challenge, especially if we took a "corporate" approach to managing it. The example is even better for planes, but not everyone has experienced being a pilot. It's easy to understand as operators of machines, systems, or organizations the importance of having the right tools and solutions to support your needs. In this case, it's all about the information you need to do your job being available at your fingertips or at a glance.

"Mechanical" dashboards are examples from the last century that show some really focused and important methods of providing information to the people that need it. They don't require you to go gather, assemble, translate or negotiate for the information when you need it. They give exactly what you need, as you need it and in a format that works. This highlights the importance of having real end-to-end data flows and dashboards that actually are connected to real information systems. The existing manually assembled Excel-based scorecards and dashboards most organizations have today are really just hiding more problems than they're solving.

Whether it's driving a car, flying a plane or running a team, department or organization, it is very apparent that information and knowledge are keys to making successful and effective decisions. The reality is that your competitive advantage and other organizational success factors are driven by the use of organizational data and information to support decision-making. The concepts of "flying blind" and "wingin' it" as an approach to reporting and decision-making will become as dated as smoking in the boardroom someday. What once was cool will be obsolete. If you focus on the Information Asset, then the tag "obsolete" won't apply to you and your career.

Over many years, organizations have had a tendency to look at IT as an expense. This makes sense if you consider the hardware, software, and operational support aspects like buying computers, paying for software, completing development technology projects, and supporting all this stuff with big, resource-heavy help desks and operations teams. Well, it's understandable that with all this, no one would really have extra time to focus on "reporting" information. But does this seem like what should be the only focus for technology management? Aren't we missing something really big?

If you step back and really look at Information Systems as they exist today, there have been many achievements and substantial progress over the past few years. With all the improvements and innovation, I believe we are nearing another special moment in technology history. I believe if someone got religion about the "I" in CIO or the "K" in CKO, they could really have an amazing impact in their organization and on their career. There's a big hidden opportunity out there today to change one key viewpoint, which is to value the Information System and Data Flow Architecture of an organization as an asset, not just as an expense.

If you run, manage or participate in an organization you can make an impact. You can easily transform the organization you're working with and enable the future. As you're aware, information drives decisions not just in business, but in all aspects of your life. Timely and accurate information has always been and will always be the most effective asset to any decision maker. Whether it is business, military, consumer, patient, etc…, information is the key to success, failure, life and death. So, if you can see the major issues that exist for information systems businesses have built and the existing approach taken toward reporting, then you understand and recognize the opportunity.

Just like driving a car or flying a plane, decision-makers need information. Why should business not utilize technology to its advantage? Data, information, knowledge, and intelligence are key assets. Let's utilize our unique ownership of these assets to build a future organizational system unlike no other. Let's build The Information Asset™, enable your future and leave your legacy.

Chapter I

Making the Case

"Get the information that people need to the people that need it. If they are looking for it on their own, you've failed."

Chapter I — Making the Case

"Get the information that people need to the people that need it. If they are looking for it on their own, you've failed."

Over the past few years, I've heard many references to the ideology that we're living in the "Information Age." I've heard this from the media, industry pundits, and web visionaries alike. Unfortunately, working on the front lines of database systems, business intelligence, and information delivery, I beg to differ with this thinking. Prove to me that I'm wrong and I'll buy the first round.

I believe it would be more appropriate to call this time in technology history "the Dark Ages of Information." I'd even go so far as to call this the "the Data Age" or something like this. In either case, I find myself hoping for a Renaissance. Don't get me wrong, I dream of the Information Age and want to live in it myself. But seeing the current condition of informational intelligence or the lack of it, I see a lot of opportunity in the future for people working in this field.

As I begin to dream of how life would be in the "Information Age," I'm often snapped back to reality when I go to work in corporate America. On a daily basis, I see how reporting really happens — everyone scrambling around, collecting data from wherever they can find it, only to deliver manufactured reports through a one-sizes-fits-all desktop spreadsheet application. Admit it, you've done it in Excel or consumed it from Excel without ever really being concerned of how the data got there.

That's right, I said it: Microsoft Excel. I know, I know… everyone has big ERP implementations, data warehouses, and robust industry reporting tools. And at this stage, almost every company today has also jumped on the Business Intelligence bandwagon — buying a tool, plugging it in, and pretending they have BI. (This "Silver Bullet Syndrome," as I call it, never works. Never has, never will.) Even with all this, unfortunately random information collection, report manufacturing and "Excel-based" delivery became the de facto reporting standard for a number of years for many businesses. To me, this is like people doing their own plumbing for every office or every cubicle. I mean, it could work, but it's kind of silly. Well, this is how people are really doing "reporting."

If you had responsibility for reporting and wanted to focus on an important business problem, then wouldn't you track down the root cause of why well-paid resources do not have the information they need to do their jobs? I can easily tell you that there are a number of obvious and valid reasons why reporting has been left to the masses to solve in any way they can. Here are some examples:

- Many big projects leave reporting until the end phases. Then when the projects don't finish on time, the reporting doesn't get delivered.

- The speed of IT departments can't meet the reporting demands of all business areas.

- Individual business areas just run with it to get the job done.

- IT departments don't have the budget or the staff to support "real" reporting groups across the organization.

- The value of good and effective reporting is not recognized as an asset, but rather as just an extension of system development.

- There's never enough time to do things right, but there's all the time in the world to do things over and over again — to troubleshoot, fix, and patch.

- Politics.

- And many more....

As much as this is a problem, this is also a major opportunity for those who have the raw insight, creativity, and focus to apply in these situations. The primary issue at the heart of all this is that no one views information or its delivery to resources as a true asset. It's just out there. There is no real true Information Asset in any business today. There is no real true understanding of what data exists, who has it, how it is used, or how it can be used.

The Problems We're Facing

It is not too challenging to understand the problems every organization faces as it relates to reporting. Just try to answer some of the following questions. For this exercise, think of any of the following that relate to you when trying to answer the questions: a company, department, group, or team. It really just depends on your current role and scope of responsibility. If that is too much, just start with one person or yourself and try to answer the questions. That should be enough to seed some thoughts and concerns.

Take the quiz:

- How many people work in your (company, department, group, or team)?
- What roles and responsibilities do each of these people have?
- What data or information does each of these people need to do their job?
- What information is available to each of these people?
- How do they get information?
- Does anyone have profiles for each employee? (What data they need, what data they use, etc.)
- What information do you need that you don't have? Internally? Externally?
- How do you find data or information?
- How's the quality of the data?
- How much time is spent collecting data?
- How much time do business people spend collecting data and manufacturing reports?
- What tools are used for reporting?
- Does anyone use spreadsheets as reporting tools — you know, where you can type in data and change numbers?
- Do you have real end-to-end reporting (where data from transactional systems is delivered to an easy-to-use and robust reporting tool that meets all of your needs)?
- What other tools are used for end user reporting?
- How do people search for data/information they don't have or need?

- How do people collaborate with their reporting?
- Do you have an effective, efficient, and responsive technology department available to you to support the reporting needs everyone has, the supporting architecture, and all of the related component solutions?
- Do you have and use metrics and KPI's?
- Do you really have any actionable data that you actively use to make decisions?
- What kind of architecture is in place to support reporting needs?
- Do you have a portal or a dashboard that meets all your informational needs? Why not?
- Does anybody care?

These are really just a handful of questions to start your mind thinking about the challenges businesses are facing today in relation to reporting. With that, if we begin to examine the issues at the individual level, this will lead us to the needs and purpose of the Information Asset.

Knowing that there are a whole host of reasons why each business has trouble with reporting, here is a list of some of the biggest issues we deal with as consumers of information from corporate information systems:

1) There is data everywhere.
2) Where's "my" data?
3) Making decisions.
4) Time and focus.

1) *There is data everywhere.*
Looking at reporting and the information systems businesses have today, the simple qualifications for these systems are that they store, process, and report data. Those are the basics. Unfortunately, as you add in the real complexities of business and technology, organizations are asking a lot more of their technology solutions. Because of these requirements and the speed of technology innovation — the data architectures, data flows and reporting solutions that most companies have today are a complete mess.

What you begin to find upon deeper analysis is lots of data stored all over the organization and used differently by different groups. It's everywhere: big corporate databases, transactional application data stores, Excel, Access, third-party applications, etc., and the painful part is that it's usually not integrated. Talk about making a case for being in the Dark Ages of Information when you try to assemble datasets to do reporting. It's almost as if all the chips are stacked against any person trying to create useful reporting. I like to refer to the information analysts as going on "Information Quests" when trying to piece together useful reports.

When someone is on an Information Quest, they are usually following a path similar to this:

- What data do I need?
- How do I get to that data?
- How can I use the data?

This is the general thinking, and is the same thought process we all go through on how to solve many problems in our personal lives and at work. Now, imagine that you're faced with the gaps, roadblocks, and inherent problems built into answering these questions. Pretty soon, you're on the phone making calls, sending emails, walking to do personal visits, and sifting through existing reports trying to get answers. Then — where to put your results as you collect them? Aha! Excel will do just fine. This is where the problem begins for every person, every day. Because of the way organizations have evolved and have just accepted that reporting is done in this manner, there are many dysfunctional reporting solutions in place in many organizations today.

2) Where's "my" data?

So now, we agree there's data everywhere. Let's pretend you start a new job in an organization with lots of data everywhere. What do you get when you start that job? A salary, basic training on processes, logins to systems, a manager, deadlines, a title . . . I think it's safe to say that almost every person in every organization has a title. Agreed? It's basically accepted that when you get a job, you get a title and a manager. These are pretty standard things today. That title has certain responsibilities and authority.

But just think for a second about the data each of these "titles," or people, needs to do their job. Oh, ok, some of it you can get from Excel spreadsheets, reports, existing BI tools, the Internet, and some you should have in your head from prior experience. That's nice, but wouldn't it make sense to really understand the data or information needed for each role in the organization — to understand the details of why that data is needed and how it's used? Wouldn't it make sense to give people access to all of their informational needs based on the title of the job that they have? Wouldn't it be effective to provide this to you when you start your job, and for every organization to understand this? I think it would.

Does the data you need exist in internal systems? Does it exist externally? Can we get it? How? These are also important questions that are limitations of every employee's reporting capabilities. Many organizations only really offer the Information Quest for you from the internal data perspective, as in, "There's finance data over there in that group. Go get it." Well, what about the concept of actually understanding and making available all internal data sources, and also integrating external data as well? I know it's a stretch based on the condition of internal information systems today, but I think it's way too valuable to leave out of the picture. At least if people had access to internal and external data, this would be a start.

The next part of your Information Quest leads you into more work in finding all the pieces. How much time does every person spend seeking pieces of information from disparate sources, only to piece together best-case metrics for weak decision-making? Seriously, how much time? Think about it. For reporting people, there is a substantial amount of time and effort applied to this phantom project.

In organizations today, no one is really delivered a map of roles or the actual profiles they have in the organization or any understanding of reporting requirements and needs. When a person starts a new job or position, they usually just get the reporting that the last person in the job got. From there, over time, they try to further assemble the applications, data, and information they need to do their jobs. Since each person in each role is doing things like this on as regular basis, just extrapolate and recognize the process that enables a substantial and consistent waste of time and money. This time could, of course, be focused in more productive pursuits.

It's interesting that corporations provide you with basic necessities like heat, water, lights, and computers, but completely ignore the information system needs of you as an individual. It's ok in the corporate world today for the data and information you need to do your job to be fragmented, misplaced, inconsistent, unrecorded, and so on, but it's a problem if you don't fill out a request form with the help desk to fix your PC. When you really look at the situation, it's very imbalanced, since many of the actions you take on a daily basis are attempts to assemble information to make decisions to help add value to the business itself. "Where's my data?" is a large, hidden and underestimated problem that can be resolved.

3) *Making Decisions.*
So if finding the data wasn't enough trouble, now comes the decision-making. In your new job, you'll be requested to make decisions. A decision is a conclusion derived from the use of supporting information or knowledge. The success of the decision is based on the results. Since decisions are made every day by every employee while conducting business, just consider how information management and decision-making occur today. Since finding the data and assembling it takes so much effort, how much time is really left to work with the data? How much time is there to transform it from raw reporting data to something useful for you or management to make decisions with? In your hypothetical new job, do you think you'll be able to make good decisions with the default reports that were left by the last person that held your job? I'm sure it's rare for people to start jobs where they're delivered the information and associated business intelligence they need to make decisions early in their tenure.

At this point, from a systems perspective, we have the databases to collect data, the applications to help manage the data, and reports to output the data. There's a substantial amount of work that can occur as part of reporting like data mining, business intelligence, analytics, etc. These are all disciplines to help support better decision-making, but are often not part of primary data flow reporting work that goes on across organizations today. This is changing, but there are big opportunities available to enable decision support reporting. Usually it is easy to tell how far along organizations have come by looking at their use of common Metrics and KPI's (Key Performance Indicators). These are usually indicators of at least some efforts to speak the same language and assist employees is making effective decisions.

Since reporting and supporting business intelligence solutions have not matured or been perfected yet, unfortunately a primary issue for organizations today is that "decision-making" metrics and KPI comparison are generally happening in someone's head. This leads to problems in repeating logic, storing and recording the logic, and associating results to decisions. Also, the reality is that these decision-makers and information consumers walk out the door every night and may or may not return the next day. How much of an acceptable organizational risk is it to have the key metric, KPI's, and decision-making algorithms only accessible in people's heads? Because of this risk and ineffective systems, it is important to really consider understanding, documenting, and managing the metrics, KPI's and decision-making contact points that exist and that are "mentally" used to run the business.

Since I could casually speculate that many decisions in organizations today are made based upon quick ideas and loosely assembled data fragments from all over the organization, how can people be expected to respond to big decisions place in front of them? Should a product manager recall a product when a defect is found? Should the Mergers and Acquisitions Vice President acquire another company? How does the director of operations communicate why and how long the production systems are down during an outage? Should the finance department hire a consulting firm to build an application? How many customers are willing to buy more products if we put these products on sale? Who are our best customers and why? There lots of questions and lots of answers that historically would just be characterized as the purpose of the people in those jobs.

Well, so back to our discussion on expectation of new employees. Shouldn't each person and role in the organization have the data they need to do their jobs? Shouldn't the organization understand the roles of the resources that work for the company and provide for that relationship? There are many resources at all levels of an organization that could benefit from better understanding of the decision-making process for each role and information required to make those decisions. How about providing each person with their own personalized portal/dashboard (user interface) on the day they start that gives access them access to all data, information and intelligence that person will need to do their job. Wouldn't you want this and expect this? In today's Corporate America I can usually guarantee heat, lights, water, and fancy coffee but when it comes to making decisions ... it appears acceptable to let this one just happen however it happens.

4) *Time and Focus.*
So if you take the exercises we described above, you can make a case that most individuals are willing to accept the fact that on a regular basis they will be searching for and assembling data rather than focusing on data analysis and real value-added decision making opportunities. This is a major issue in most organizations. The time and focus of resources as it's related to reporting is weighted toward searching, assembling and reconciling rather than really analyzing, translating and effectively using the information. I believe there is substantially more value to be gained from the latter and also by using intelligent/actionable information to make decisions. It's just unfortunate that many companies and managers believe in this concept but regularly fail to implement the proper solutions to get it done.

So again, let's make the case that you start as a new employee but we apply the Information Asset solution to the mix. When you start, you immediately are given an informational overview of the organization: the data available, what it is, and how to get it. The data, the information, the intelligence you need are all part of the show. Instead of running around and trying to manufacture reports, you are given a portal that has access to all the transactional systems, reporting, and information interactions you need. Your security profile ensures you'll able to see all data related to your role. You also get direct access to metrics and KPI's that you're responsible for with drill-to-detail and pivoting capabilities. On top of that, we'll add alerts and notifications for key problems or issues that can be identified and displayed for you immediately. How great would it be if you were not searching for data or living as a prisoner in the cells of Excel? I know for sure you'd be in a much better position to begin using and managing your data to translate it into information and intelligence to support your decisions and impress your new boss. There's lots more we could talk about in this example, but I think you get the picture. With all this, I'd say maybe now you'd be working in the Information Age on your way to the Intelligence Age.

Addressing the Issues

So how does a person, a department, or a company address the issues and really begin to utilize the data they've been collecting for a number of years now? The reality is that the company needs to begin to focus on the solution and then allocate the time to get there. Time and focus are the key drivers that will lead you down the following path:

- The Transformation
- Crossing the Bridge
- The Information Asset ™
- The Recipe: Building The Information Asset

   The Information Asset solution and the Recipe will be discussed in detail in Section II. But to get to the solution from where you are today, you will need to recognize the Transformation and Cross the Bridge.

The Transformation

Reporting is a very generic term that carries with it a certain understanding of information being extracted from a system and delivered to a user. The term "reporting" had been used for many years, and has generically referred to basic reports delivered from transactional systems. With all of the related information technology progress over the years, the term *reporting* has evolved to encompass many different types of extractions and many different types of delivery and use. In recent years, the term has really expanded to a whole new range of deliverables, including: datasets, OLAP cube-based reports (from data warehousing), scorecards or dashboards, and portals. Throughout this book, I'll make references to reporting and try to qualify the specific type as needed.

As much as the term *reporting* has carried forward with the same core concept intact, it's important to understand that the actual content of reports has changed. The original content or the base requirements for reporting have always been data — just raw data from applications. With the sophistication of data warehouses, data marts, ETL solutions, and business intelligence, we're living the evolution of the Data Maturity Scale™. As data moves through the data flow architecture, it is transformed. The transformation and maturity scale are shown below:

Data Maturity Scale

These are maturity factors based on reporting that businesses cultivate over time. A transformation occurs to data as more logic is applied over time. So in most businesses today you'll see a majority of the reporting still done based on data and information. Raw data is the easiest one. Just collect data and report it as-is. At this point, everyone has data and many ways to collect it, but not everyone has information, knowledge, or intelligent data. As you add more layers of transformation with clear requirements, you can address this deficiency. As we work to transform your business with the Information Asset, most people in the organization could benefit from doing reporting with knowledge and decision intelligence instead of just using raw data and basic information.

Usually, all of this recognition of utilizing data and translating its value is currently happening in small organizational pockets or in someone's head. The importance of the different stages of maturity outlines how the data transformation can become more valuable to end users. A key to addressing this is really recognizing and referencing requirements with the understanding that raw data starts as such, but matures as it makes its way through the architecture.

It's important to recognize and plan effectively for ensuring organizations are finding their way to the utilization of more mature and sophisticated representations of their data. We'll be covering this general topic a lot throughout our discussions on the Information Asset. Once you understand the main issues, the transformation and how we reference reporting, then you're ready to cross the bridge from the issues to the solutions side.

Crossing the Bridge

Crossing the Bridge is a metaphor for transitioning organizational focus from software and technology projects to really understanding the architecture, workflow, roles, metrics, and culture of the organization. The length and width of the bridge are all relative to your organization. For some companies, this task will be easier than others. For others, this change might be a daunting and even unachievable objective. Standard roadblocks do apply, as everyone around you will not immediately be onboard with where you're going. But in any case, Crossing the Bridge will be a primary objective for you to begin you efforts in creating the Information Asset.

This journey will be taking you over a road that has never been traveled before in your organization. I can easily draw a parallel to the Lewis and Clark Expedition to explore the American West. You'll need to have financing and formal backing, but you won't have military cover if you run into trouble with the locals. Your life may not be on the line, but your career may be. It is the road less traveled because the reality is that building the Information Asset could never have been done before in history. This historical perspective will be discussed in Chapter II – the Stage Is Set.

To help the organization cross the bridge from where it is today will take perseverance and a thick skin, but hey, what change doesn't? In the end, it will be a small cost for leaving your legacy. And when you are successful, which I know you will be, you will be afforded the notoriety and celebrity of mapping the frontier and adding incalculable long-term organizational value. So the choice will be yours: Cross the Bridge to the future, or live in the Dark Ages of Information.

The Solution and Recipe: The Information Asset™

What is it? Chapter III will cover in detail the definition and components of the Information Asset, and Chapter VI will give the Recipe of how to implement it. The most important context to have is that the Information Asset will set a strong data flow architecture foundation, build a Decision Intelligence Model™ on that foundation, and provide the best solution delivery and support system to transform your organization from where it is today to a world-class knowledge-driven icon. Your role in this as described in this book will be to understand the concepts and deliver the Information Asset to your organization. The second part of your exercise will be to migrate the organization from the mess of disparate data sources and haphazard reporting to world-class business driven by the utilization of the Information Asset and an intelligence-driven workforce.

The Information Asset solution will enact many shifts from current thinking and approaches that exist today. Some of these are outlined below.

- Based on many of the issues we discussed above, I think it's apparent that many organizations are missing a complete end-to-end data flow architecture. Also absent is the understanding of their informational and intelligence needs and effective people and processes to keep the engine running. I know this can be built and I know it should be built. You might say, "Isn't this business intelligence?" I would answer that business intelligence is too generic to define what we're talking about. We need business intelligence software and concepts as parts of our solution. One good thing is that if you try to implement a real BI solution, the exercise will help you uncover the requirements that would identify the need for the Information Asset.

- The Information Asset is very obviously absent in most organizational structures today. Since the responsibility of this concept falls under the CIO/CKO management area, people in these roles would have the most to gain from moving down this road. I remember seeing the roles of CIO/CKO showing up in many organizations a number of years ago. For most of what

I've seen, people in these roles just took over responsibility of technology projects and operations management that nobody else wanted. I've never really seen a CIO or CKO enact changes that would create long-term organizational value. I expect the Information Asset to change that and move the CIO/CKO role from the technology and operational hangman to the Commander-in-Chief of the circulatory and nerve centers of the organization. The Information Asset focus can really transform their responsibilities and allow people in these roles to reach their intended potential.

- Generally, IT departments have been focused and are usually measured on very technical terms, like software and hardware installations, operational processing, report development and related software, and hardware solutions. What about business value? This is not usually an area of measurement because it's too subjective to measure for IT. It's usually easier to complain when the hardware is down and you can't run a report that a user thinks is very important. How about if the CIO/CKO was measured on the value they could provide to the business? Move the operations piece out of the puzzle and now focus on business value with information, knowledge, and intelligence. Now we're on to something — something that's not happening today.

- For many years, hardware and software solutions have been put in place in organizations to store and move data. This is a unique point in time when all of these previous efforts can be leveraged to utilize the existing solutions, build a strong and scalable data architecture foundation, and deliver value from reporting and decision intelligence solutions.

- Basically, the Information Asset will be a living part of the organization. In building the Information Asset, you'll begin to learn about concepts like:
    o Understanding and documenting organizational roles.

o Finding and documenting the KPI's/Metrics "gold nuggets."
o Designing a complete information delivery platform.
o Recognizing and correcting data gaps.
o Creating a roadmap to move from problems to solutions.
o Measuring success along the way.

The Information Asset consists of three primary components:

> **The Foundation: Data Flow Architecture**
  o Hardware/Software
  o Enterprise Data Model/DW
  o Enterprise ETL
  o BI Reporting Platform

> **Decision Intelligence Model™**
  o Organizational People/Roles
  o Informational Interactions
  o Metrics and KPI's

> **Solution Delivery and Management**
  o End-to-End Data Flow (Uninterrupted and self-managing)
  o Self-Service Intelligent Reporting
  o Experienced and Knowledgeable Information Consumers

Summary

With all of these things in mind — Tough Questions, Where's My Data, Decision Making, Time, and Focus — it's clear that the current state of IT in companies and IT management is not delivering on these needs. I believe the world of information technology projects today is very hit-and-miss as far as focus and effectiveness. If you reference information technology projects, you might think of some initiatives like:

1) Creating Business Intelligence Reports for Marketing.
2) Building a data mart or Data Warehouse for Finance.
3) Upgrading Oracle from 9i to 10g.
4) Comparing MicroStrategy to Cognos.

Sound familiar? These are common and useful efforts, but usually fall way short of what technology has to offer. These are worthwhile projects, but none of these ever consider the value of the Information Asset and importance this has to the success of people and the company on a daily basis. Taking on a purpose that defines and utilizes the Information Asset has substantial value that transcends most conventional thinking.

Be advised: the Information Asset is not a project. It's not a software solution. It's also not an assessment or an objective. It is a way of life and complete change as to how data can be stored, transformed, utilized, and managed to really solve business problems and add core business value. It's a commitment to something groundbreaking.

No matter what level you are, you can have an impact with the Information Asset. Solving the issues we discussed above does not need to happen at the top level in an organization. Building the Information Asset can be implemented for a whole company, a department, or even just a small group. So if you're CIO, CKO, department manager, Technical Architect, or Programmer — you're in a position to really make an impact using technology to help your organization.

If you are open to being enlightened and loosening the life-inside-the-box chains that bind you, I think you'll be ready to make an impact for yourself and your organization. Through this book, I will provide you with the direction, the recipe, and the drive to move yourself, your company, and your customers out of the "Dark Ages of Information." You will soon be on your way to designing and creating not only a solution, but a longstanding legacy for yourself by understanding and creating the Information Asset. Building the Information Asset could be one of the most important organizational objectives you've been a part of. This is a unique time in technology, and the stage is set for those ready to take on the challenge.

Chapter II

The Stage Is Set

"Chance favors the most prepared."

Chapter II – The Stage Is Set

"Chance favors the most prepared."

I'm sure you've heard the old saying that luck is where preparation meets opportunity. Well, call it luck or not, this is a special time in technology history. No matter how creative, intelligent, or technology savvy you are, you could not have defined and built the Information Asset at any other time in history. There are just too many dependencies on the technological innovation and progress over the past few years. The opportunity has basically been enabled by all of the technology solutions that have evolved before this point in time. The key primary enablers we can reference are data warehousing, the Internet, portal technologies, and business intelligence reporting.

It's similar to the concept of how you could not create and run a company like eBay in the 1980s. Without the Internet and ecommerce technologies, it was an impossible idea. Remember life in the office without email? Remember your personal life without cell phones? These are all very similar to where "reporting" is today and how life will be different in organizations when they have data architectures to move information and reporting platforms to deliver decision intelligence.

Basically, at this point in time, the stage is set for a big organizational shift. Business intelligence software is driving forward the interest in making use of data and creating useful information. BI software vendors are putting forth products that drive people to try to build business intelligence solutions. What in turn happens is that these software product implementations just end up shining the spotlight on huge deficiencies in the existing data flow architecture. What becomes obvious when trying to do business intelligence this way are issues like poorly designed data models, inflexible and short-term focused ETL solutions, bad data quality, lots of data and business rule fragmentation, lack of BI reporting skills, etc.

Most of these deficiencies are not based on lack of foresight, but are just circumstantial based upon how new this stuff is and how quickly organizations have been forced to adapt to the changes. With the understanding that there are many details that could be discussed in this section, I will focus on a high-level overview of the key components that set the stage.

Historical Building Blocks

1) Hardware and Storage
   The increase in raw hardware processing power and disk storage has enabled the base foundation for all of the software solutions that sit on top of these. There have been many companies involved here like HP, Sun, IBM, and Dell on the hardware side, and EMC and Network Appliance on the storage side. All of these innovations have basically enabled more and more data/information to be processed, stored, and delivered.

2) Relational Database
   With the relational databases of the 1970s, we saw the seeds of the future. Companies like Oracle, Informix, Sybase, and IBM all competed heavily into the 2000s to own this piece of your architecture. This is an absolute core architectural foundation component.

3) Transactional Applications
   As I remember, the race was on in this space for much of the 1990's. Many legacy transactional applications already existed from the 1970s and 1980s as "green screen" applications. Dumb terminal applications ruled the world for some time, but were painful to work with because they were usually proprietary and challenging to integrate. Then came the promise of client server with pretty GUI front ends and relational database back ends. This was all the rage, and everyone was involved in projects like ERP and CRM implementations. This very competitive industry segment is still important today, as these applications are often primary source systems. Some key companies in this race were companies like SAP, Siebel, PeopleSoft, and Oracle.

4) Data Warehouse/Data Marts
   Where do we put all the data we're collecting from all these transactional systems? Let's store it in a database

and call it a warehouse. Sold. Once again, these types of solutions were really happening in the late 1990s. People began to see the value of keeping their data, formatting it in different types of data models to support historical analysis, and then breaking down the warehouse into more digestible sections called data marts — which ended up being subject area data warehouses. All of these efforts are the drivers for better methods of querying databases, working with large datasets and looking at datasets as cubes. Some of the companies that offered modeling tools to build these solutions and data analysis tools to do this reporting were companies like IBM, Oracle, Informatica, Brio, SAS.

5) ETL (Extraction, Transformation, Load) — aka Data Processing and Data Movement
This one makes sense, too. It's how we get data from the transactional databases to the data warehouse. This moving and processing became popularly known as ETL, and software vendors starting selling ETL platforms. In the 1990s, there were many projects focusing on data warehousing and ETL. Not everyone was buying ETL tools at the time because they really were not mature enough. A majority of these efforts were custom efforts with languages like PL/SQL and PERL. Some companies that developed early ETL software solutions were companies like Sagent and Ascential.

As we'll see, ETL solutions are even more important today than they were in the early days because the data processing and movement requirements have grown within each company. With more and more data, transformations, and consumers of data, ETL solutions are as critical and relevant as ever.

6) The Internet
So then it happened in the late 1990s: the Internet changed the world. Of course, it changed the world in many more ways than one, but for us it created the ultimate delivery medium. We were no longer tied to desktop software to do reporting. We now had a simple thin client browser with an abundant and open range of new development and deployment options. There are many derivatives of the base Internet that spawn as children and act as important

components; these are discussed separately in the next few items. The software companies that initially had an important role for us were Netscape and Microsoft. The browser wars were an interesting time.

7) Web Applications/Ecommerce
As you know, the Internet enabled software applications to be built on a new platform, and also enabled commerce on this new platform. This in itself opened a whole new world of opportunity for every business. The landscape of business completely changed with transactional web applications.

To sell products, you no longer needed to build a physical store. There are books worth of information on this topic, but there are two key enablers here for us. These enablers are that we now could have applications enabled to run through web browsers and also reporting enabled to run through browsers. This is a big deal because this solved many deployment, upgrade, and support issues with software from the client server and previous eras. With transactional and reporting web applications enabled, for the first time in history we were be able to assemble complete solutions for users that included components from each of these areas and deliver them to anyone, anywhere. Leaders in early development here would include companies like Amazon.com, Yahoo!, and eBay.

8) Application Server
From the transactional applications, ecommerce, and related solutions, we saw the need arise for another key server technology other than the database server. The application server made its entrance in the 1990s to meet a variety of needs.

From handling Web traffic to being the primary piece of middleware to run all applications, this component is positioned to serve many purposes in different architectural configurations. The application server in all of its flavors runs Web, Web apps, ecommerce, business intelligence, search, multimedia, etc. However, each company implements this tier of the architecture differently. In any configuration, this technology is still a core component to the base architecture for everyone.

Some key companies driving the direction in this area were BEA, IBM, Sun, and Oracle.

9) Portals

In the early 2000s, the Internet platform and the concept of "portals" sparked a new way to deliver information, applications, and reporting. This new solution approach took the form of a dashboard similar to what you see in cars and airplanes. It was a design approach assembled utilizing Web technology and a new application design perspective. The concept started with Internet sites like My Yahoo!, where you had "your personal portal" with small representations of portlets, or widgets, like email, weather, stocks, and links to more info.

This concept then spread to businesses where internally you could see projects, budgets, email, search, and other functionalities. Out of this, you saw the development of collaboration solutions, dashboard and scorecard solutions and other related portal-based functionality approaches to software development.

With the initial portal software technology, it was apparent that this would be the future for both reporting and applications. Everything you needed would be at your fingertips and be accessible from any computer at any time via the Internet. There was no turning back; portals have also changed the world — well, at least my world. LOL. Some companies focused in this space: Plumtree, Business Objects, Cognos, Oracle. As you could guess, companies focusing on this software ended up selling business intelligence software solutions using this functionality. It's a logical transition.

10) ODS – The Operational Data Store

Along the way, as businesses gained experience with data warehousing, they realized a subset of the data needed for operational purposes was best suited for their own databases. This makes a ton of sense from a processing and performance perspective, so we started to see the concept of an Operational Data Store showing up in Entity Relationship Diagrams (ERDs). I have to say this is one concept that I find very straightforward, but I have seen it cause much confusion in organizations. Correctly building a separate database design for specific purposes often helps with scalability and long-term direction of the data architecture.

11) Data Analysis Tools
When data warehousing and data mart projects were popular in the 1990s, these data analysis products really became important software tools. Everyone was looking for easy-to-use ways to query and report, better approaches to working with large datasets, and functionality or capabilities that were more self-service focused than existing reporting tools at the time. Many software solutions popped up to handle data analysis/OLAP-type requirements. These tools introduced concepts like data cubing, pivoting, drilling, and interactive graphing to name a few. The primary drivers in this toolset were ease of use, performance, and self service. If you tried reporting from a data warehouse without these tools, things often got ugly.

Because these tools have maintained their positions in organizations since that time, you'll often notice that these data warehousing tools were basically relabeled and recast as business intelligence tools. It was subtle, but it happened. Similar to portal software, the following are some of the companies involved in this area: Brio, Oracle, Hyperion, Cognos, Business Objects, MicroStrategy.

12) Business Intelligence
Business intelligence software was derived from a number of the above items, and has been a primary reporting focus of many organizations in the 2000s. As described above, two of the primary dependent technologies used in BI solutions are portal and data analysis technologies. At this point in time, BI has really become the primary marketing vehicle for many companies to sell database, ETL, portal, and data analysis solutions into the enterprise. Business Objects, Cognos, Hyperion, Oracle, and MicroStrategy are some of the big names here.

13) Universal Search, Content Management, and Multimedia
Some of these other concepts have also evolved from the Internet and subsequent iterations of applications developed with it. These are important to note because they will enable functionality for your Information Asset related solutions. For example, there are many different

33

types of content like data, images, pictures, and videos that may need to integrate with your transactional or reporting solutions. Also, data is currently stored in many different technology formats — database storage, email servers, file systems, filing cabinets, etc. All of this content needs to be managed and also to be searchable. These are important pieces of the big picture, and will need to be recognized to completely account for all aspects of organizational information and knowledge.

14) Single Sign On and Security Models
One final area for discussion is the concept of Single Sign On and the Security Model. People, profiles, logins, access levels, data security and all related topics are important components of the solution design for the Information Asset. Background and understanding of progress in these areas will help create very stable and secure solutions. Over the past few years, many of the above discussions have adjusted direction and deliverable compliance based upon Sarbanes-Oxley and terrorism concerns. This also can be a very big discussion in many areas, but for our purpose, a very powerful security model enabled through the software technologies above will provide for a safe and secure solution.

I could go on and on in each of these areas, but I know there are many books and other information available on these subjects. Our purpose in reviewing these key components is that all of these innovations and solutions have set the stage for building the Information Asset.

Summary

Reviewing all the progress that has been made over the past few decades, you can't help recognize the huge potential that's out there in the information technology area. To begin to capitalize on the opportunities, you'll need to recognize the components of the solution and the approach to deliver it. We'll cover these topics in the following chapters, starting with defining the Information Asset and then proceeding to discuss the components in detail. With the history overview we just went through, you're now ready for that discussion.

Chapter III

The Information Asset™

"Information is the blood of the organization."

Chapter III – The Information Asset™
"Information is the blood of the organization."

As blood flows through our veins to supply all parts of our body with required nutrients and life, it is relatively the same for information systems and organizations. Data and information are basically the blood of the organization. Ideally, data flows through organizational systems to supply all resources and downstream systems with required information to support decisions and enable the businesses to operate.

With the understanding of how critical blood is to the body, it would be fair to say that data and information is of equal importance to organizations. Since your body makes sure the blood you pump to your organs is consistently on time and pure, wouldn't you also expect the data and information that's delivered to all resources in your organization to be effective and valid as well? This seems to make sense, but in many cases today organizational data is not treated with the importance of what blood is to the body. The associated data flows I've seen could be described in terms of the analogy, as the blood is often polluted, the nutrients don't show up when expected, and when good blood does show up to organs, it can't be used effectively because it can't be trusted. I think if the current leadership and approach that is taken with information systems were applied to a human as per the analogy, the patient would not have much time to live. I think organ failure would happen quickly.

Hopefully this example has tuned you in to the importance of building the Information Asset. This endeavor will essentially involve designing and constructing the intelligence delivery or circulatory and nervous systems of the organization. In this design, it's very important to fully understand all the organs or resources, the roles they play, and what information/nutrients they require to perform their jobs as expected. Most companies today are focused on various pieces of the puzzle, but not the complete solution.

With the understanding that data and information are the blood of the organization and the information asset is the circulatory and nervous system, there's short and long term value to making this a priority. Just pretend for a second that you stopped collecting, storing, transforming, and reporting data in your company; how long do you think you could continue to compete in the marketplace? Ok, let's also pretend you just keep collecting and storing data in big databases, but do not apply any logic or intelligence in attempting to report on the data. In either case, these thoughts seem silly, but are relative extrapolations of what is happening today in many organizations. It's like flying sophisticated airplanes without the cockpit instrumentation panel while wearing a blindfold; might be fun for a few minutes, but the ending is going to be painful.

At this stage in technology history, we know that our information systems are not at the level of sophistication of the human body's circulatory or nervous systems. But the comparison does provide an interesting frame of reference. I believe there is real hope in creating information systems and data flows as sophisticated and effective as the circulatory system. I also believe there's hope in creating a Decision Intelligence Model™ within organizations that is as intricate and effective as the human nervous system. That's why we're talking about the Information Asset™. It's a major change in the current approach to database systems and business intelligence that recognizes the importance of data, information, knowledge, and intelligence. This new approach raises these ideals from the operational cutting room floor to a level with true value and lasting respect. Give an organization a reporting solution and they'll come back every day for more, but build an information and intelligence delivery system into the core infrastructure of the organization and you will enable the continuity of data delivery and intelligent decision-making for years to come. That's the legacy available though delivering on the Information Asset.

With this in mind, it's very rare that you'll see company or department management engage in a project that is truly visionary and can add real lasting value to an organization, employees, and shareholders. If you work in a corporate business setting, you probably have gained a good understanding for the way business really operates. It's not always the most visionary or value-added projects that get top priority. Rather, you can count on politics, short-sighted management decision-making, and budgeting constraints to drive managers to operate in their comfort zones — unable to

37

break through the status quo and focus on really valuable initiatives. More often than not, management and companies in general enjoy working on safe projects with short-term goals in mind. Being agile is one thing, but stringing together years of short-term-goal focused projects as an architectural solution is disastrous.

Without visionary projects, it's also challenging to keep people engaged. Unfortunately for most technology workers, the environment they work in forces them to spend most of their time involved in process and politics rather than adding real value by applying technology to solve business problems. In many cases on the technology side, you'll most often see the focus on projects center on hardware, software, and/or software development. Sometimes you'll even see a major focus on just hiring the right talent or "good" people. These are good and useful, but by no means visionary or lasting; they are almost just basic survival necessities if you work in technology today. So if you're committed to building the intelligent information delivery architecture, then you'll also enable an intriguing magnet to hire, engage, and retain talented technology professionals.

Being a visionary or a leader in technology management is the road less traveled for many reasons, so therein lies the opportunity. It's not often in the history of business that all the planets align and present you with a huge opportunity (discussed in Chapter II — The Stage Is Set). If you're ready to take on the challenge and initiate the most valuable organizational effort of the new millennium, then you've come to the right place. Building the Information Asset has that purpose — a mindset and direction that can transform your organization from ordinary and reactive to groundbreaking and inspiring. At some point, there comes a time when somebody needs to be a leader and sail over the horizon without fear of falling off the face of the earth.

What is The Information Asset?

In simple terms, the Information Asset can be represented as an equation. This is a good high-level starting point and reference to use as we make our way into the details.

The Information Asset™ Equation:

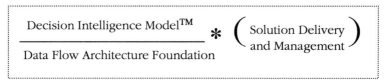

$$\frac{\text{Decision Intelligence Model}^{\text{TM}}}{\text{Data Flow Architecture Foundation}} * \left(\begin{array}{c} \text{Solution Delivery} \\ \text{and Management} \end{array} \right)$$

At this level it is pretty simple. Now, if we review that equation in a little more detail, it would look something like this:

The Information Asset ™ Equation (Detailed):

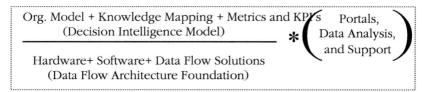

$$\frac{\text{Org. Model + Knowledge Mapping + Metrics and KPYs}}{\text{(Decision Intelligence Model)}} * \left(\begin{array}{c} \text{Portals,} \\ \text{Data Analysis,} \\ \text{and Support} \end{array} \right)$$

$$\text{Hardware+ Software+ Data Flow Solutions}$$
$$\text{(Data Flow Architecture Foundation)}$$

These equation representations basically outline the primary components that make up The Information Asset™. As we progress through the next few chapters, we'll be discussing all of these components in great detail. By the end of our discussions, the equation examples should make complete sense and provide a good mental crutch to help summarize many details. Let's begin to look into some more detail on the primary components.

The Information Asset™ Component Overview

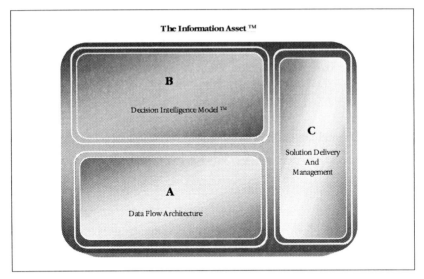

Figure 3.1

The Information Asset™ consists of 3 primary components:

A) <u>The Foundation: Data Flow Architecture</u> (Figure 3.2)
The supporting data flow architecture enables the collection, storage, movement, and transformation of the data and information and is the critical foundation component. This foundation supports the Decision Intelligence Model™ and Solution Delivery.

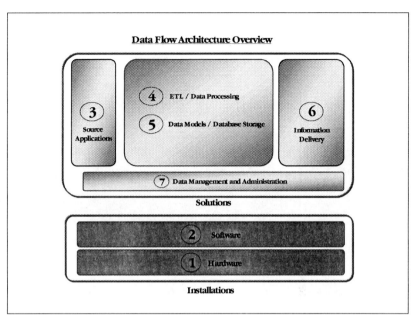

Figure 3.2

B) Decision Intelligence Model™ (Figure 3.3)
A primary goal of the Information Asset is to drive decision intelligence methodology through the organization. This involves understanding the organizational structure, the informational needs of the people and roles in that structure, and the key metrics or Key Performance Indicators (KPI's) that are required and used to make decisions. A description of each of these subcomponents is listed below:

1) **Organizational Model** — defines all of the roles people have in teams, groups, departments, and across the entire organization.

2) **Functional Knowledge Mapping** — maps the people/roles to informational interactions and associated needs and requirements.

3) **Metrics and KPI's** — defines all the Metrics and Key Performance Indicators (KPI's) that are used in the department, company, and industry.

4) **People** — the actual resources who work in the organization.

41

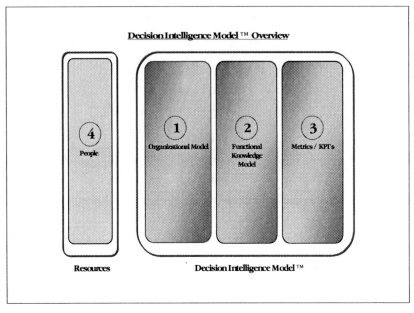

Figure 3.3

C) <u>Solution Delivery and Management</u> (Figure 3.4)
With the foundation in place and a solid understanding of the decision intelligence information requirements, this area enables the software reporting platform functionality and associated processes that provide the consistent and flexible delivery of information and intelligence to decision makers. The primary focus of this component is the portal and data analysis concepts discussed in detail in Chapter 5 — Solution Delivery and Management.

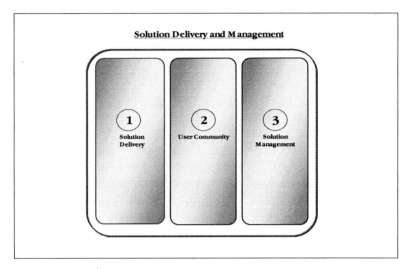

Figure 3.4

If you'd harnessed the internal hidden value to be found in the components above, you would be in the most agile and nimble position available to any business today in reference to reporting and decision-making capabilities. You could adjust, turn, and make decisions with pinpoint accuracy and without fear because you'd have all the required informational support to justify the actions. Your "reporting" or analytics resources could be focused on purely value-added activities. By building the Information Asset as defined above, you would really be creating a tangible physical asset and enabling a brighter future for your company and your career. All the pieces together are not just a solution, but a real and true asset.

At a physical level, basically companies have always been defined by their combined assets. For instance, every company has buildings, office furniture, hardware, software, people, capital, etc. These entities are assets and collectively define the company. Another array of assets that help define a company are tangibles like secret recipes, algorithms, and chemical compounds (i.e. ingredients for Coca-Cola or something like Google's search algorithm). These types of assets really define what a business is and how it operates. You might be able to conclude that the combination of these types of assets defines every company. But, in every business today, there are also other assets that I believe are even more important than a building, a formula, or the people employed at any given point in time. These assets are the roles, metrics, and knowledge that are utilized by people constantly — to do business, make decisions, and attempt to take actions that will support the best interests of the company. In these areas, you rarely see consistent focus to document, utilize, and take advantage of this most precious and unique asset — the "Information Asset."

Even with all these other tangible assets you rarely hear anyone speak of this primarily intangible, but very important, asset — the knowledge used to make decisions or even the value of a powerful and scalable complete data flow architecture. There are so many decisions made up and down the organizational chart on a daily basis that truly define the short and long term success of an organization. That's why the project of defining and building the Information Asset is truly invaluable to an organization and the people in it.

This representation may sound simple, but the concept of the Information Asset doesn't exist today. Sometimes simple but obvious inventions go unnoticed until they're thrown into the spotlight. I'd make the case that building the Information Asset was not even possible until now. To even begin to put all the pieces together, you and your team really need to understand the ins and outs of business intelligence and the other supporting concepts before you can really see the biggest picture of all. Many companies are just going through BI implementations for the first time as you read this.

Asking the Tough Questions

With a current understanding of your department or organization today, try answering some of the following questions:

From a business perspective:

1) What roles exist?
2) For each role, what decisions are made on a daily basis?
3) For each decision, what information is used to make the choice?
4) Where does all of that information come from?
5) Is any important information missing?
6) Can you get the missing information?

7) What decisions were made for each person and each role over the past year?

From a technology perspective:

1) What are the components of your data architecture?
2) Do you have an end-to-end data flow for analysis and reporting?
3) How much of your user community uses Excel as the reporting delivery interface?
4) How much of your enterprise data is stored in Access and PC tools?

These are very interesting questions that are often not easy to answer because nobody has spent time to determine or document the answers and keep the information up-to-date. It's almost a wonder how companies can sustain success and long-term growth without general and consistent understanding of how their business is really being conducted. Answering the questions above are really just fundamental exercises, but these exercises and the related project work can be used to save substantial resource time and add a lasting asset to any organization.

I remember presenting business intelligence and portal concepts at conferences events in the late 1990s and early 2000s. It took a lot of effort to get through to certain audiences on both the technical and business sides with the new concepts, but when the light bulb turned on in each of those people, it was great stuff. Today, I no longer need to explain that business intelligence is more than just writing reports. It's interesting to see the progress that's been made technically and emotionally in the industry. It's an even more exciting time now to put all the pieces together and build something as groundbreaking, important, and lasting as the Information Asset.

When we begin to put the technical architecture puzzle together in Chapter IV, we'll discuss many details about data flow architecture and how the Information Asset defines and utilizes this foundation component. From the decision intelligence and solution delivery perspective, in future chapters we'll also discuss the details that make up these areas. One important consideration to review before we dive into those details is the understanding of where your department or organization is today from a decision intelligence maturity

45

perspective. By this, I'm referencing the work and progress that's been done up to this point in your information technology reporting areas. Before you embark on building the Information Asset, it's important to have a clear understanding of where your organization is right now in reference to decision intelligence capabilities.

As shown in Figure 3.5, every organization progresses through levels of maturity over time as they attempt to utilize business intelligence concepts and subsequently recognize real business value from reporting. This maturity scale is shown and outlines the maturity and progress that is needed to achieve decision intelligence capabilities. The work requires a mix of good people, process, and technology projects over time and follows a very logical and natural maturity cycle. When you're at the top of the steps looking down, it's a great place to be. Each department or group in a company can really chart its own progress on a scale like this; it's not just for the complete organization.

Decision Intelligence Maturity Scale

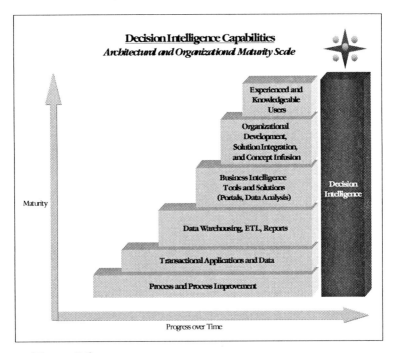

Figure 3.5

Examining the scale from bottom to top, you will see that the basic business solutions start us off. Business starts with people following basic processes and recording those transactions in simple transactional systems. As they gather data and want to keep history for analysis and use, they then progress up the scale into the world of data warehousing, ETL, and reporting. From there, the logical progression is to begin enhancing reporting with business intelligence tools and associated solutions. The first efforts in creating business intelligence solutions usually more mimic basic reporting than real value-added "business intelligence." This is primarily because users don't quite understand the concepts and can't really generate good requirements.

What happens next is interesting. There is a substantial amount of time and effort that it takes to work with resources at the next level. There is a lot of people and process work to do developing BI skills, integrating real BI into their existing reporting solutions, and introducing methods and infusing the concepts with internal and external user communities. This type of work moves beyond basic business intelligence and into the concept of decision intelligence. These people and process efforts drive the ability to generate better requirements and utilize the BI technology for more effective reporting and the subsequent creation of actionable and intelligent information to support decision-making.

Well, after all of that, you'd make it to the final step. All of the work from the previous steps can now occur with experienced and knowledgeable users. This enables great design and development sessions and the proliferation of useful and valuable requirements. In the long run, this reduces the substantial rework that is required with an Excel-focused user base, so from this spot on top of the maturity staircase we are in a great place. This is a position where we can cycle content back into the architecture to create better efficiencies for the ongoing development of new solutions and maintenance of existing reporting solutions. Talk about a point to stop and smell the roses.

So, as we embark on defining, building and implementing the Information Asset, take into account where you're starting from. If you're struggling with transactional applications and data warehousing, then you have a much greater distance to travel than if you've been running BI tools for a few years. In either case, I assure you that with the proper time, focus, and determination, we can get you to a happy place.

Summary

Understanding the definition and purpose of the Information Asset is an important first step in solidifying the mechanics of what it is and how to make it work. In the following chapters, we'll drill down into more technical details on the data flow and solution delivery components. Technical knowledge in these two areas will prepare us for the decision intelligence and recipe discussions in Chapter VI — "The Recipe" Building the Information Asset. So, if you're willing to get your hands dirty and look under the hood, let's go to Chapter IV and check out what a good data flow architecture looks like.

Chapter IV

The Foundation:
Data Flow Architecture Components

"A chain is only as strong as its weakest link."

Chapter IV – The Foundation: Data Flow Architecture Components

"A chain is only as strong as its weakest link."

I once heard a story about engineers in ancient Rome. Basically, engineers would construct bridges to expand the road system for the movement of troops. To ensure the quality of the bridges, the emperor would ask that, upon completion, the engineer stand underneath the bridge while the legions marched across the top. I found this to be a funny yet valuable lesson in the approaches available to ensure the quality of infrastructure projects.

An approach such as this might actually help a lot in today's technology world, where we don't see a lot of really true quality architectures we can depend on for the long term. These types of projects are usually budgeted, staffed, and measured for success only in the short term. And then, after management makes many poor short-term decisions, people usually begin leaving the organization. It's usually easier for people to just leave a company for greener pastures when the problems pile up and the operational wildfires rage within the architecture. Well, the good news is this is one of the primary issues addressed by the Information Asset. The data flow architecture is a critical foundation component, and will directly enable any real success we can deliver with reporting and decision intelligence solutions. Because of the nature of the Information Asset, we will be dependent on the underlying architecture components and will need to build long-term solutions to address tactical and strategic needs.

At this point, we've covered a lot of the background that leads us to building the Information Asset. With an understanding of what the Information Asset is, it's now time to dig deeper into some of the more technical aspects to understand the data flow. As per the issues and dependencies shown in earlier sections, it's important to really walk through and outline what the data flow architecture is and review all of the components. What we will be looking at and discussing is the foundation for the Information Asset. If the foundation is in good shape, our job will be that much easier. If it's been pieced together over the years, the scope of the foundation-related work will need to expand to address all of the issues.

Through my involvement in business intelligence implementations over the past few years, I have witnessed how important the data flow architecture is to the success of these types of projects. On many occasions, middle management is often squeezed into the Silver Bullet Syndrome by business and upper management demands. They are sold on the concept that you plug in BI software and you'll automatically just get fancy dashboards with lightning-fast performance. You know, cross your fingers and hold your nose — everything will just work and will be perfect. This never happens. One thing I can guarantee that will happen the first time around — these types of projects always end up magnifying issues and gaps in the data flow architecture that need to be addressed.

As much as I've tried to help this process along in certain situations by having deep detailed discussions, writing the issues and areas of concern in memos, and just plain pleading with customers and management not to underestimate this, it never seems to impact existing expectations. It's almost like telling a teenager not to do something or to be careful. Just as someone might advise in this area, sometimes you just need to inform and let nature teach the lesson.

I think it's a right of passage for every company to go through the first project and realize that the success of BI implementations is completely dependent on the entire data flow architecture. If the existing ETL solution doesn't handle errors well and just blows up regularly, then the data regularly doesn't show up in your fancy BI tool. If you don't have validation built into your database models or ETL, then customers regularly get information that is often incorrect. Over time, users will learn not to trust the reports they get through your fancy BI tool and they'll start doing their own thing again. If you have a poorly designed data model, then chances are that you'll have performance issues as you try to scale and manage larger datasets with your new tool. As much as I'd like to go on and on with this topic, I think you have probably lived through these types of issues already and understand all too well.

So, with all this said, the discussion then turns to "Well, how can we do BI?" And as much as it hurts to say it, the answer is that you need to build a long-term data architecture to support the organizational data flow. The existing quick-and-dirty solutions pieced together over the past few years just won't support where you need to go. The example I use frequently in conversation is that of building a house. The BI implementation is analogous to painting and decorating a second-floor bedroom of a house. Usually what happens is the following: as a contractor, I walk into the house and the manager (not the owner) says, "Hey, I want you to spend 50k on decorating some bedrooms/bathrooms upstairs with state-of-the-art decorations and features. Everyone in my neighborhood is doing it, and the paint and decorating sales guys gave me good deals if I bought their products this month."

Ok, so as a decorating contractor, of course I'm excited to get this contract. When I go into the house to assess what's happening, I start to find there are bigger issues. I turn on the water and immediately a pipe bursts and floods a room. I try the lights and they start blinking like crazy. I examine a wall and see a ton of termites enjoying the woodwork. I check the basement and see huge cracks in the foundation. There's also no working heat or air conditioning. In seeing this, it's apparent there are bigger issues here. As a professional, I can't just ignore what I've seen with the primary systems of the house and try to decorate one or two rooms as agreed. Some contractors would happily ignore these concerns. So, when I bring up these concerns with the manager or even the owner, what's the response? Usually, it's just, "Well, can't you simply patch the pipes, turn off the lights, buy termite traps, patch the foundation, and then just do the rooms? The answer could be yes, but we would not be addressing the major issues and would just be continuing to hide them. This is like leaving grenades in the house as you leave after beautifully finishing two bedrooms. With this situation, as soon as the rooms get finished, how could someone enjoy beautiful and perfect bedrooms when all of the supporting infrastructure is falling apart and may blow up at any time?

Well, that's almost exactly what happens with BI. The bedrooms are business areas, and all the supporting infrastructure is the data flow architecture. As much as it's fun and exciting to focus on slick BI reporting solutions, the reality is that those solutions are dependent on many core foundation components. These components of the data flow architecture need to be working correctly, and need to be positioned to support all the needs of the solutions built on them. If this is not the case, then why spend time and money on the BI solutions or the fancy bedrooms when the value will not be realized?

The key point of the example is that when trying to do business intelligence projects and when building the Information Asset you will need a stable and scalable foundation to utilize and realize the value of the effort. Many people will try to tell you otherwise, but there are not many places to hide if relevant information is not available, not correct, and not delivered on time. Quick-and-dirty may have gotten many companies to today, but it won't support tomorrow and the information delivery architecture requirements that are coming. Keep this in mind as we walk through the components.

Primary Components

The primary physical components of the data flow architecture are:

1) Hardware
2) Software
3) Data Flow Solutions

Since hardware and software are standard technology practice areas, these will not need to be covered in as much detail. As you're aware, there are many vendors and configurations, but base functionality and purpose will remain the same for our discussions.

Hardware /Software
The hardware and software installations enable the creation and support of the solutions. The underlying work to select, install, configure, manage, and administrate hardware and software installations is important, but the real value we need to discuss is defined above this at the solution level. The following is a general list of the hardware/software installations and environments you'll need to have in place to support the required solutions. This is a quick checklist to make sure you have all the major pieces:

- Transactional Applications/Source Systems
  (There will be many of these...)
- Database Server(s)

- ETL Tool/Platform
- Application Server(s)
- Business Intelligence/Reporting Platform
- Data Management Tool/Platform
- Development Tools
  - Case/Data Modeling
  - SQL Developer
  - Java Developer
  - Etc.

Data Flow Solutions

The value or pain every organization feels often sits in the actual solutions that are built using software installations. I've seen firsthand on many occasions that it was easier for middle management to blame a software product as the problem rather than recognizing and taking responsibility for poorly designed solutions.

From a reporting perspective, our primary concerns are the solutions that support the data flow. The primary data flow solution components are the following:

- Source Applications
- The Enterprise Data Model and Data Warehouse
- The Enterprise ETL Solution
- Business Intelligence/Reporting
  - Standard
  - Data Analysis
  - Portals/Dashboards/Scorecards
- Data Management

As we reviewed in Chapter III, Figure 4.1 shows a diagram outlining the primary component areas and their reference to the data flow architecture.

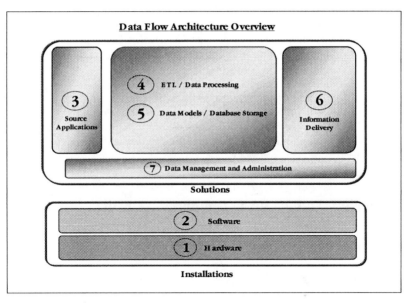

Figure 4.1

Component Descriptions:

1) **Hardware** – All physical networking, servers, computers, and related storage to support software products and solutions.

2) **Software** – All physical software products required at various stages of the data flow to support solutions with differing functionality and purpose.

3) **Source Applications** – These are all of the source systems or applications that collect transactions on a daily basis. These source systems are sometimes referred to as OLTP or transactional applications. Every business has many of these types of applications, e.g. ERP, CRM, Budgeting, HR, Manufacturing, Feeds, etc.

4) **ETL/Data Processing** – The movement and processing of data from end-to-end in the data flow.

5) **Data Models/Database Storage** – The database model design, the associated database objects that support all database requirements, and the data itself as it's stored in the objects.

55

6) Information Delivery – The software tools and methods used to deliver the data and information to the user community with reporting and business intelligence solutions.

7) Data Management/Administration – Applications and API's (Application Programming Interfaces) to assist in the data maintenance, supporting module maintenance, administration, and reporting solution support.

Data Flow Architecture – Component Details

To gain a better understanding of the data flow architecture components, it will really help to discuss some of the key component details and subcomponents for these areas. In the following pages, we'll review these subcomponents through the use of diagrams and basic models. These diagrams may appeal to the more technically oriented reader, but will provide anyone with a great blueprint to use to map back to their work. Each diagram is also filled with enough detail to initiate a lot of discussion and would require a substantial amount of time and effort to describe in detail.

Since there are many books written on each of the various topic areas, I do encourage you to seek out more information in each area that interests you. My primary focus is to present you with overview introductions to each of the areas to show the complexity, importance, relevance to the Information Asset – data flow architecture.

Let's start by looking at breakdown of how the primary component areas will be referenced in upcoming diagrams. Each diagram will be labeled with a Level as described below. The Level label will orient you as to how high- or low-level the diagram's content describes.

Level 1 :   Overview
Level 2 :   Component Detail
Level 3 :   Subcomponent Detail

Data Flow Architecture – High-Level Overview (Level 1)
The best place for us to start is to look at the high-level logical overview of all the components that exist at the solution and data flow level as shown in Figure 4.2. This overview outlines

the key components of the architecture with some data movement details. The diagram makes reference to logical architecture and outlines representations of moving data from source systems to reporting.

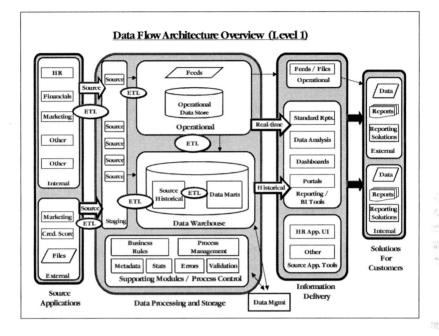

Figure 4.2

Data Flow Architecture — Key Components (Level 2)
When looking at the overview, it provides a good blueprint for finding the areas for which you need more information. It's important to review key component areas in more detail to understand some of the concepts. I've identified some key components to include in this section. Again, the idea is to open important areas of interest for further discussion and research.

These are the following key component areas to review at a more detailed level from an architectural perspective:

1) The Enterprise Data Model/Data Warehouse
2) The Enterprise ETL Solution
3) Information Delivery

1) The Enterprise Data Model/Data Warehouse

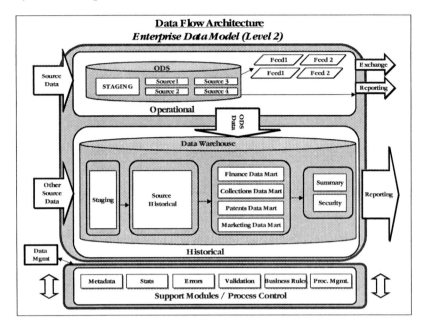

Figure 4.3

The Enterprise Data Model and Data Warehouse are keys to successful data architectures. Many organizations have often tried to build this complete solution but have not been successful. This area is a critical solution to support the Information Asset and needs to be represented successfully.

Here are some of the primary components and concepts:

Component Descriptions:
A) **Staging** — Area for storing all incoming data to support processing and reprocessing needs. (Performance-focused)
B) **Operational** — Area for storing operational data.
   1) Source — Data stored to meet operational source system requirements. (Integrity-focused)
   2) Outgoing — Data stored to meet operational reporting and feed requirements. (Reporting-focused)
C) **Data Warehouse**
   1) Source Historical — Data stored for the whole organization for all of history. (Integrity-focused)
   2) Data Marts — Data stored to support reporting needs by area. (Reporting-focused)

3) <u>Summary</u> — Data stored to support reporting aggregate needs. (Performance-focused)
4) <u>Security</u> — Metadata stored to mange security and individual profiles.

D) **Supporting**
1) <u>Metadata</u> — Supporting description data for all components.
2) <u>Stats</u> — Supporting statistical data for all data movement.
3) <u>Errors</u> — Supporting error data for all data movement.
4) <u>Validation</u> — Supporting validation data for all data movement.
5) <u>Business Rules</u> — Supporting business rules data for all data movement.
6) <u>Process Mgmt.</u> — Supporting process management rules for all data movement.

The data warehouse component is a big piece of this puzzle. Taking the concepts down one more level for the data warehouse, we begin to see the physical implementation concepts as shown in Figure 4.4.

<u>Data Warehouse Design – Level 3</u>

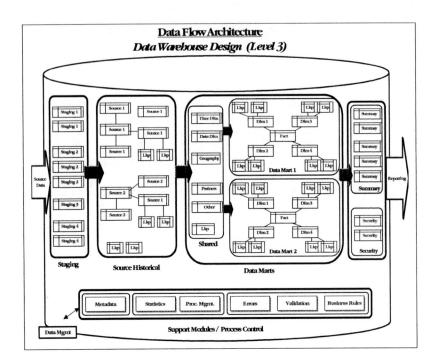

Figure 4.4

Once again, there is so much to talk about here, I'll continue on with the understanding that there is a lot to learn about building data warehouses correctly. If the concepts shown in the diagram are foreign to you, then this may be a good area to consider for additional research.

2) The Enterprise ETL Solution

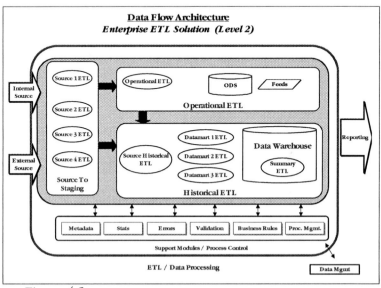

Figure 4.5

The Enterprise ETL Solution is also a critical element that can make or break the entire data flow architecture. There are so many important components of this solution that most of the reporting success is often dependent of the success of this solution. This solution's primarily responsibility is to properly refresh all the data, information, and intelligence — as efficiently and effectively as possible.

Many organizations try to build this complete solution, but are often not successful because of short-term focus and lack of proper investment in this area. This lack of value recognition often leads to a lot of time and resource commitment focused on fixing and troubleshooting rather than just spending the money up front and doing it right the first time. This area is a critical solution to support the Information Asset that needs to be analyzed or certified. Any identified issues must be addressed.

61

Here are some of the primary components and concepts:

Component Descriptions:
A) **Processing**
    1) Source to Staging
    2) Staging to Operational
    3) Operational to Source Historical Data Warehouse
    4) Source Historical Data Warehouse to Data Marts
    5) Data Marts to Summary
B) **Business Rule Processing Engine**
C) **Process Control Management**
D) **Supporting Modules**
    1) Error Handling API
    2) Statistic API
    3) Validation API
    4) Metadata API
E) **Data Management**
    1) Reporting Data Maintenance
    2) Supporting Module Maintenance
    3) Data Flow Administration
    4) Business Rules

3) Information Delivery

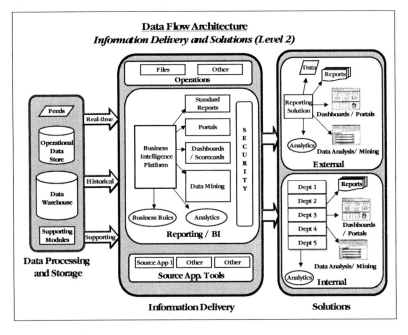

Figure 4.6

Users need a *fast* and *easy-to-use* "*tool*" with *flexible access* to *relevant data* that helps them do their jobs more efficiently and effectively. This delivery-focused section of the data architecture enables the integration of the database and ETL with the BI software technology to provide the best solution for end users. This is the area where we're really able to take advantage of the best software technology to supply the best reporting and business intelligence solutions.

Component Descriptions:
A) **BI Reporting Software Platform**
    1) Standards Reports
    2) Data Analysis
    3) Portals
        a. Reporting
        b. Transactional
        c. Collaborative
    4) Scorecards/Dashboards
    5) Analytics
    6) Business Rules
B) **Self Service Capabilities**
C) **Security Model**
D) **Reporting Profile Management**

Summary

We've really covered a lot of ground in this chapter. The Data Flow Architecture is a critical foundation for the Information Asset and is inherently complex and technical. Completely understanding, documenting, and addressing issues in these areas will help you be more successful in the long run with any reporting, business intelligence or Information Asset work. With this understanding we'll now be able to move into discussing how to utilize the Information Delivery platform and build effective solutions. Now, let's dive deeper into the technology concepts and direction of our Solution Delivery components.

Chapter V

<u>Solution Delivery and Management</u>

"A fully-integrated and intelligent portal on every virtual desktop."

Chapter V – Solution Delivery and Management

"A fully-integrated and intelligent portal on every virtual desktop."

Long story short, this is the finished product you deliver. With all of the supporting components before it, this area covers the actual end product people use and interact with on a daily basis. End users, power users, executives, managers, internal customers, external customers, and whomever you decide to deliver to, this is end product they see, know, use, and judge you on. With this understanding, you could see how important the data flow architecture and decision intelligence models would be in delivering effective, useful, and valuable reporting solutions. Once you've delivered these solutions as described below, management of these will then become just as important to continuously adjust to the technology changes and business needs over time.

On the solutions side of information delivery, there are two primary solution concepts that comprise everything we need. These concepts are portals and data analysis. The following discussion provides you with more background and detail in these areas. These are important to discuss because business intelligence software technologies always have at least these two primary pieces of functionality. We will utilize each of these for delivering decision intelligence through the Information Asset.

Here's an overview of these concepts and functionalities:

A) Portals
- Single point of entry to various types and levels of information and information interactions.
- Organized, pre-defined, and usually aggregated data for reporting.
- Dashboard format (Quick glance = immediate answers).
- Drill and link capabilities.

B) Data Analysis (multi-dimensional)

- Ad hoc analysis.
- Pivoting and drilling to detail.
- User-defined formatting, printing, graphing capabilities.
- Crosstab summarization and analysis.

Portals

Portals are the user interfaces that provide a platform for business intelligence and beyond. I'm sure, at this point, that you've heard of portals, scorecards, dashboards, etc. These concepts are primarily web-based solutions with user interfaces or web pages called "portals" composed of smaller web pages called "portlets." Each of these portal pages usually exists within a tab structure and/or link-based structure. This allows each portal application to consist of many portal pages by category with many different portlet types and styles. Each portal page has a unique composition.

Here's an example portal page which gives you a general idea of the look and feel:

Figure 5.1

Portal solutions allow many different types of work to be accomplished with one primary user interface. Figure 5.2 shows an example of the concept of having one user interface present your world to you through one unified solution.

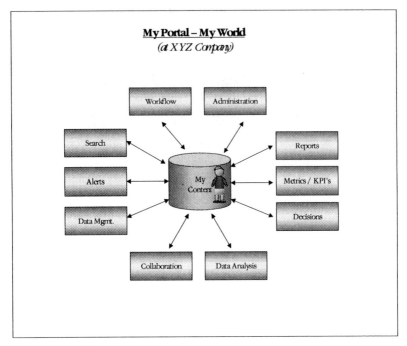

Figure 5.2

Portal Composition
Portals are very powerful and very flexible. They are composed of many portlets with a wide range of different types of content, styles, formats, purpose, etc. Some examples of portlets and content types are shown below and in Figure 5.3.

- Source:
  o Internal/External
  o Content-Based
  o URL/Link-Based

- Functionality:
  o Reporting

68

- Static — Informational
- Aggregate
- Intelligent — BI
- Data Analysis
- Pivot and Drill-to-Detail
  - Collaboration
  - Data Management/Transactional
  - Administrative
  - Application
  - Process Alerting/Control/Audit
  - Search

- Format:
  - Charts
  - Graphs
  - Grids
  - Widgets
  - Content-driven

- Frequency:
  - Real-Time
  - Almost Real-Time
  - Historical
  - Forecast/Prediction

- Content Types:
  - Data
  - Images
  - Sound
  - Video

- Secure:
  - By Login
  - By Profile

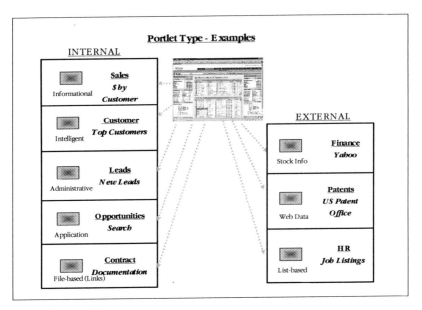

Figure 5.3

Portal Types

Along with the many different types of content and portlets a portal page can have, there are many different types of portal pages that can exist. Usually the portal page type is derived from the purpose and use of the pages(s). Obviously, the types of the content on that page help define the type of portal. Some examples of different types are listed below.

Portal Types

	Functional *"Marketing Portal"*	❋ Data specific to Functional area ❋ Informational / Intelligent Portlets
	Operational *"Cost Center Manager Portal"*	❋ Data specific to User / Role across Areas ❋ Informational / Intelligent Portlets
	Administrative *"Budget Administrative Portal"*	❋ Data specific to an application ❋ Administrative / Application Portlets
	Application-Based *"Bonus Compensation Portal"*	❋ Informational / Application Portlets ❋ Some data is updateable and maintained ❋ Links related to data and application components are common
	Dashboard *"CEO Portal"*	❋ Data from all relevant organizational areas ❋ Data is aggregated and allows for drill down ❋ Intelligent Portlets

Figure 5.4

The roles, responsibilities, and information interactions defined in the Decision Intelligence Model will help define the portal, portlets, and portal solutions required. As this stage, it's just important to know there are various types of these and that there is substantial development flexibility in meeting needs of every role and every person.

Portals and the Organization

There is no question that the Internet and portal software technologies changed the face of what we can do with business intelligence. Portals play a critical role as the primary delivery medium for the Information Asset. Once you've developed some portal solutions, there is a bigger picture that presents itself as you gain momentum.

In working with many organizations and seeing how they have implemented portal technology, it's usually easy to get an understanding of where an organization is in reference to the use of portals in the organization. Shown in Figure 5.5 is a maturity that outlines the progress steps each company takes on the journey.

71

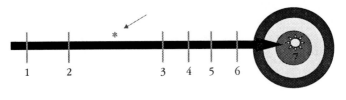

Organizational Portals
Maturity Scale

1) Intranet / Website
2) Advanced Intranet * *Many organizations are here...*
3) Business Intelligence Reporting Model
4) Operations Functionality (Transactional)
5) Collaboration (Email / Calendar / Scheduling)
6) Fully Integrated "Desktop" – Process, cllaboration and Intelligent Reporting
7) Metric-Focused / KPI-Driven Information Management

Figure 5.5

Maturity Scale Stages:
1) **Intranet/Website** — Basic website and intranet.
2) **Advanced Intranet** — Very sophisticated intranet with departmental segmentation and advanced web features.
3) **Business Intelligence Reporting Model** — Effective dashboards and scorecards
4) **Operations Functional** — Transactional enabled processing and integrated business intelligence.
5) **Collaboration (Email/Calendar/Scheduling)** — Integrated workflow processes and systems.
6) **Fully Integrated Desktop** — All information interactions through your portal.
7) **Metrics-focused/KPI-driven information management** — Decision Intelligence focused delivery and management of knowledge and intelligence through your portal and across the organization.

Through portal implementations and as the solution matures, opportunities open up to support portlet and data services. This is more tied to a service-oriented architecture. The hierarchy and portal representation would look something

72

like what is shown in Figure 5.6. Each department would be contributing portlets and data services into a common pool for use and reuse across the organization. With this model, the organization can leverage all development across the organization over time. This is an important aspect for each organization as they mature with these technologies. At this point for us, it's just important to reference this idea to support efforts in the data flow architecture area.

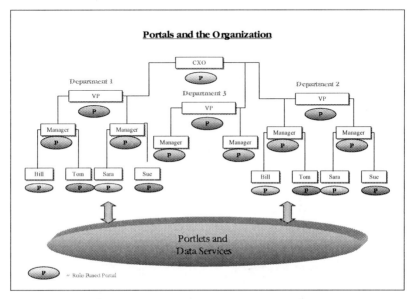

Figure 5.6

With all of this work in the right direction, portals can become the most effective and critical solution delivery vehicle for any organization. Building and managing these solutions with a "big picture" approach over time will enable many cost-saving and effective process and reporting integration opportunities all along the way.

Along with portals, the other concept functionality component enables us to really analyze and "slice-and-dice" the information. I refer to this as "data analysis capability."

73

Data Analysis

The other primary component needed from a BI platform perspective along with portals is a data analysis tool or functionality. Data analysis is sometimes also referred to as data mining and can be traced back to tools that were built to support easy and useful access to data warehouses. These tools are absolutely required and are primary components in reporting delivery. The primary features of these tools are the ease of use, self service, pivoting, drill-to-detail, and scheduling/summary features, to name a few. In most BI tools today, the portal and data analysis features tend to blur together, but it's still important to discuss the raw features separately because each technology relates uniquely to the Information Asset delivery mechanisms.

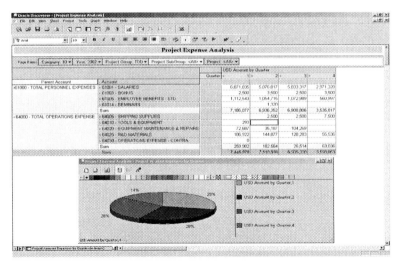

Figure 5.7

Primary Components:
1) **Self Service** — User-friendly interface with many user management capabilities.
2) **Page Detail/Pivot** — Ability to pivot on any data elements.
3) **Drill-To-Detail** — Ability to drill to any detail level to find answers to questions.
4) **Crosstab/Matrix** — Ability to crosstab or matrix any dataset.

5) **Filtering** — Full conditioning and filtering options.
6) **Scheduling** — Report scheduling and management.
7) **Interactive Graphing** — Robust graphing and charting all active datasets in reports.
8) **Post-Dev Logic** — Ability to add programming or grouping logic to data elements.
9) **Summary** — Performance summarization capabilities.

Solution Management and Requirement Promotion into the Architecture

As you build your solutions and deliver them into your user communities, an important focus for the continued success of these solutions is proper management. A way to ensure the solutions are managed correctly is to make sure the creative development done by power users or end users is captured, understood and worked into the existing solutions for all to use. Once your data architecture, report delivery mechanism, and solutions are working well, it's important for you to regularly and consistently promote progress back into the architecture or core solutions. Some example of these types of requirements or creations could include business rules, calculations, metrics, groupings, new KPI's, etc. You'll see each of these being developed and tested in the field over time.

For example, if someone decided to create a reporting grouping called Color Category: Cat A = red, blue; Cat B = orange; Cat C = green, yellow. Let's say this is a very useful and important grouping in a company. This grouping, once found, shouldn't be allowed to stay out in the end-user world because over time we would see multiple people creating this logic. New requirements or creations derived "in the field" need to be captured and rolled back into the existing architecture to be integrated with base solutions and made available for others to use. This is a people, process, and technology combined directive. Figure 5.8 outlines this process.

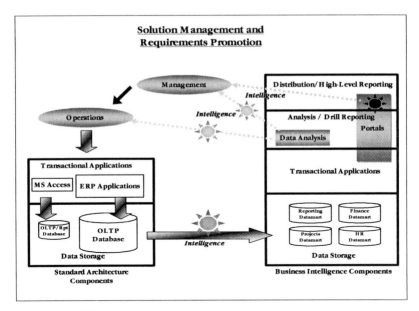

Figure 5.8

Key Processes

Along with the promotion of requirements and development of creations back into the base solutions, we have some other processes that are also very important for solution management. Keep in mind that these key processes will be required to manage your solutions by addressing issues and maintenance while continuously striving for the highest quality experience and deliverables for your users:

1) **Requirement Promotion** — Moving field creations back into core solutions (described above).
2) **Development, Testing and QA** — This is a standard development methodology process.
3) **Release** — This is also standard and supports continuous and effective improvements.
4) **Reporting Request** — User-focused process to allow for development assistance.
5) **Reporting Support** — User-focused process to allow for production support.

There are always many processes that can be implemented to assist with ensuring the solutions are managed effectively. These are just some of the primary ones for you to keep in mind.

Summary

Portals and Data Analysis are key concepts and solution components that need to be utilized in solution delivery. When these concepts are coupled with a great data flow architecture, this combination is a very powerful aspect of the Information Asset. If you are ready to start down the road of progress, let's discuss the Recipe. Once you have the Recipe, you'll have what you need to begin to make a difference. Laying out the goals and objectives is the first step.

Chapter VI

"The Recipe"
Building The Information Asset™

"Build it and they will come. Don't build it and they'll go somewhere else, or each one of them will try to build something like it themselves..."

Chapter VI – "The Recipe"
Building The Information Asset™

"Build it and they will come. Don't build it and they'll go somewhere else, or each one of them will try to build something like it themselves..."

Well, if you've made it this far and the challenge hasn't scared you away, then you are ready. Put on your business and technology chief hats, because we're ready to plan and to build the Information Asset, knowing we have many obstacles to overcome. As with any major efforts, defining where you're going and why are important first steps. Let's start with our Goals and Objectives:

Goals/Objectives:

Goal
Create an Information Management and Delivery system and supporting culture known as "The Information Asset™" that understands the roles people assume in the organization, defines the information contacts points and metrics/KPI's for each of the roles, and provides for the effective and consistent delivery of the relevant knowledge and decision intelligence required to support decision-making.

Objectives
1) Define, document, understand and implement the Decision Intelligence Model™.
   A) Determine and document the roles people have in the organization.
   B) Understand what information and knowledge each role requires to do its job.
   C) Determine and document all informational interactions for each role and associated people with that role.
   D) Determine the Metrics/KPI's that are used by people, departments, organizations, and industries.
   E) Translate Metrics and KPI's into useful, actionable, and intelligent information for each role and each person.

80

2) Create the Information Asset Roadmap to identify and plan all projects needed to update, fix, or build all required components for the solution.

3) Conduct and deliver on integrated projects in the following key areas:
   A) Data Flow Architecture Projects
   B) Decision Intelligence Model Projects
   C) Solution Delivery and Management Projects

4) Provide for and support the foundation and end-to-end data delivery and information management system with organizational sponsorship, including people, process, and technology.

In following through on our goal and objectives, we'll be proceeding to build the Information Asset as shown in Figure 6.1.

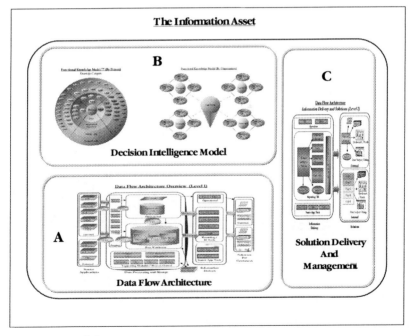

Figure 6.1

The Recipe

This is it, the value and the vehicle for your legacy. The Recipe that follows is a series of Stages with exercises and objectives you'll need to follow to take your organization from where it is today to a new level of understanding. You will embark on the creation and documentation of a previously intangible gem and vision of the future.

Following the Stages and Steps will lead you to delivering the solution. Note: You can do the exercise for a group, department, or the whole organization. I always recommend starting small and building prototypes or pilots to gain proficiency and momentum. I'll reference the full organizational examples as we walk thru the steps with the understanding that you're probably starting smaller with a team or department. If you get the concept and agree on the purpose, any approach of the work will take you to the same destination.

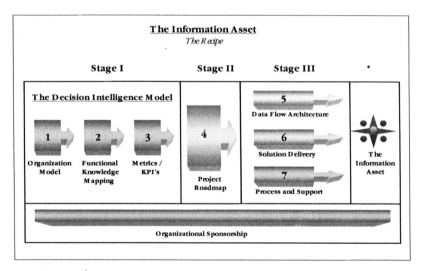

Figure 6.2

Stage I: The Decision Intelligence Model ™

Understanding The Organization (like never before...)

Stage I is all about understanding the team, department, or organization like never before. No one has ever taken the time to understand:

- The roles each person has.
- The informational interactions each role has.
- The functional knowledge mappings for each role.
- The Metrics and KPI's required for each interaction and mapping.
- The decisions made by each person/role and the results of those decisions.

There are three primary requirements gathering exercises in Stage I:

    1) Create the Organizational Model/Map
    2) Create Functional Knowledge Models
    3) Document Metrics, KPI's, and related decision points.

Once we have completed the analysis and documentation for these three areas, we will finally have a very valuable representation of how this organization uses data, information, knowledge and intelligence. We will have something that has never existed before. The resulting requirements we have collected will basically be a blueprint of the nervous system of this organization. With this blueprint, we will have the understanding and requirements we need to update, fix, or develop the data flow architecture and the solution delivery components. The quality of this work will drive the quality of what can be delivered by the Information Asset. Are you beginning to see how this understanding can be a real tangible asset after all?

Let's start with the first step, the organizational model:

1) Create the Organizational Model/Map

Creating the Organizational Model/Map is the first step in making a difference. This step is actually one of the easiest steps because most organizations have organizational charts that generally lay out the titles and people hierarchy. The only real exercise will be determining the roles and responsibilities for each title. For example, the Director of Product Development may have the following roles and decision-making responsibilities: Department Manager, Project Manager, Cost Center Manager, Process Approval Manager, Technology Lead, etc. As you begin the exercise, you'll recognize that many of the same roles exist and are shared across the organization.

The end result of the exercise is a matrix of the people/titles with the roles and responsibilities for each. When finished with this exercise, you will have a living document that is the first requirement for the Information Asset. You will have outlined the departments or groups and the related roles of the organization that are needed to operate business on a daily basis.

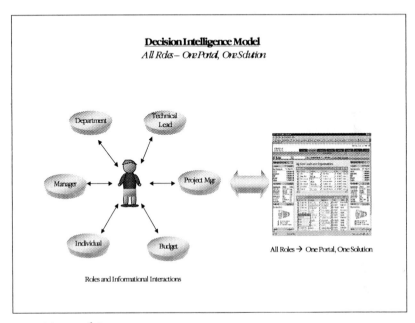

Figure 6.3

As you document each of the roles, you'll be on your way to assembling important mapping information for the upcoming exercises. In the end, we'll have enough information defined to build useful and effective portal-based solutions for reporting and information management. As shown in Figure 6.3, with each person we will be able to conduct business through a primary and complete information management and delivery system using a portal interface.

The Tasks below outline the approach for gathering information on the organizational model:

Tasks:
1) **Clearly document all Department and Job Title Levels:**

Departments

Finance
Human Resources
Technology
Marketing
Etc.

Table 6.1

Job/Title	Levels
Chief Executive	10
Vice President	9
Senior Director	6
Director	4
Manager	3
Etc.	2

Table 6.2

2) **For each Department in the organization and for each Job Title or Level, document the roles.**
Here are some examples:

Title/Level	Roles/Information Categories
Executive	Overall Vision/Direction
	Overall Organizational Mgmt
Director	Department Management
	Department Direction
	Budget and Expenses

Manager	Team Management
	Budget and Expense Compliance
	Staffing/Resource Allocation
	Purchasing
	Project Oversight and Support
Technical Lead	Design and Build Solutions
	Run Technical Teams
Project Manager	Project Tracking
	Project Deliverables
	Project Management
Business Relationship Manager (BRM)	Business Area Initiatives
	Request Management
	Project Management
Common — Employee	Payroll
	401K/Benefits
Etc.	Etc.

Table 6.3

If the roles have never been documented before, you may face some challenges, but as you work your way through the exercise, you'll be adding value no matter how challenging it is. Once you have completed these two steps to clearly outline the organization, you're now ready to attempt the functional knowledge mapping.

2) Conduct the Functional Knowledge Analysis and document Functional Knowledge Model™

In Step 1, you completed the organizational model. You might say Step 1 is a much easier exercise than this one because everyone usually has organization information from an organizational hierarchy and payroll perspective. Once you have a clear understanding of the basic departments, titles, roles, and related informational categories, you'll be ready for this very important exercise. With this exercise, we'll start finding out information that's never been organized and documented. We will be finding all the informational contact points that drive decision-making for each person and each role he or she plays. You'll really begin capturing information no one else in the organization has captured before. It will definitely be something everybody can use.

Functional Knowledge Model™ (By Person)

Conducting the Functional Knowledge Analysis (FKA) and then building a Functional Knowledge Model™ (FKM) for each role in the organization is the next step. Remember, you're looking for all information interactions, including reporting, content management, and transactional interactions. To do this correctly, you'll need to work directly with each individual to do this mapping. Face-to-face conversation and dialog is absolutely required. For each person and each role, you'll be producing something like this:

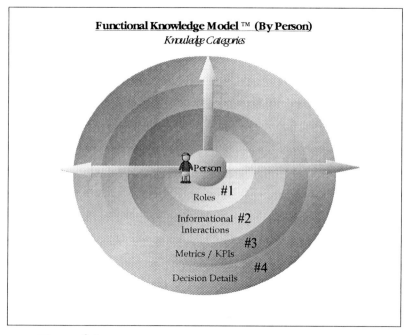

Figure 6.4

Using the roles identified in the previous exercise, you'll be capturing three main requirements with as much detailed information as possible for:

1) Roles (from Step 1)
2) Informational Interactions/Contact Points
3) Metrics/KPI's

2) Document Decision Details for each Metric and KPI.

In the next very important step, you'll need to take each of the metrics and trace them to decision-making thoughts. A very basic example worksheet might start something like this:

Metrics/KPI's	Decision Details
Number Labor Hours Available	I need to determine and communicate hours my resources worked by week so that planning and scheduling can be done for upcoming weeks.
Labor Cost	I need to keep watching my labor cost because if my resources are over-utilized I will need to communicate this ASAP.
Budget vs. Actual Variance	I need to see on a daily where I am in reference to my budget and expenses. My job performance is measured on the success of keeping this variance close to 0.
Project Progress to Estimate Alert	I need to be alerted when my projects are missing milestones and deadlines.
Issue Status and Aging Alert	I need to see issues that have aged and not been addressed. I need to follow up with resources on these issues.
Resource Utilization %	I need to see the utilization of resources on a daily basis to manage how each is deployed and schedule future projects and work.
Etc.	Etc.

Table 6.5

Please note: This is a very detailed, complex, and lengthy exercise. To get inside someone's head and understand how they think and why they need certain information is not easy. You may need many worksheets and find different effective ways to record this information. The bottom line is that anything you can gather is better than what you'll have when you start.

3) Document Security Profiles each Person/Role.

Now, to complete our Functional Model, we'll just need one more primary piece of information — the Security Profiles. To document a profile, we'll need to take the roles we defined above and map back to all the people who have that role. For each person, we then need to list specific data sets they can see. This will provide us with the information needed to finalize the profile design and security mapping.

This can also be a very detailed exercise, because for each person in each role, we need to understand metrics, datasets, reports, and the details that make up that person's unique profile. This information will outline exactly the data grouping by element that each person can see for each role they are in.

Here's an example of a worksheet for this exercise:

Roles	Person	Security Profile
CFO	Ed Elverson	Cost Center: All Resources: Susie, Bob
Manager	Susie Jones	Cost Center: 345 Projects: 11, 25, 36 Resources: Charlie, Tom
Manager	Bob Stevens	Cost Center: 201 Projects: 22, 16 Resources: Ann, Bill, Mark

Table 6.6

Completing this exercise will finish the steps needed for the individual FKMs.

Functional Knowledge Model™ (By Organization)

As you begin to capture all of these details for each individual, you'll start to see clear Functional Knowledge Models forming. At the end of the exercise by individual, you should have a very good Functional Knowledge Map for each person, but also a broader organizational understanding. From that understanding, you can then take and expand the FKMs to represent groups, departments, or organizations. This is the place where science meets creativity. The results might look something like the model shown in Figure 6.6.

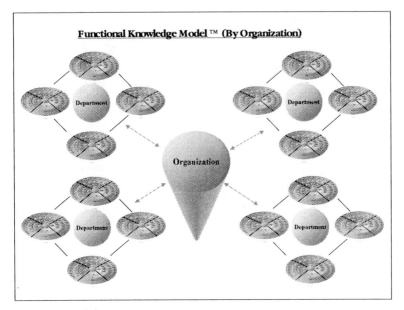

Figure 6.6

The exercise to create a Functional Knowledge Model™ for the entire organization will be a monumental achievement. This work could take years to complete, but when finished it will provide the organizational blueprint for decision intelligence and the primary design for solution delivery. As you try to assemble this information, you may learn more about how people work and interact with their data. Let's look into some details of this.

Types of Informational Interactions
As you gather requirements, you'll begin to notice that different roles have different categories of informational interactions. Your analysis will dig deep into each role to understand the knowledge contact points, including the reporting, transactional, and content management interactions for each. Through this exercise, here's a general overview of the types of interactions you might see and try to record:

1) Reporting and Data Analysis
    a. Decision Intelligence
    b. Alerts/Action Indicators
    c. Reviewing Information

d.   Drilling to Details
e.   Analyzing/Data Mining
f.   Support for Decision-Making
2)   Transactional
    a.   Entering/Updating Time and Expenses data
    b.   Entering/Updating Budget data
    c.   Managing Security Profiles and data mart Lookup tables
3)   Content Management
    a.   Entering/Updating Portal Content

Depending of the type of responsibilities that exist for each role, you'll see some roles as transactional-heavy while others are all reporting. Of course, there are some roles that will have a fair mix of all three. Within every organization, the transactional-heavy portals most often exist at lower levels in the organization and reporting-heavy at the upper management levels. Figure 6.7 shows an example of how the requirements might be distributed at different levels in the organization.

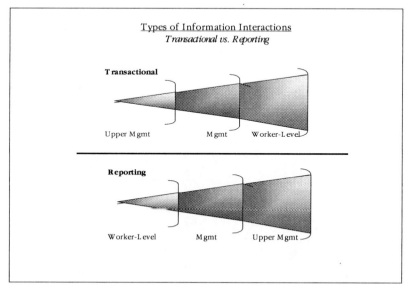

Figure 6.7

Different types of interactions can easily be integrated into one solution by using different portlet types. If you're willing to consider the finished product of our information delivery mechanisms to be a portal for every person with access to all their information needs, then this will be easy to accomplish. In many cases transactional, content management, and default reporting portlets are available from source applications and software solutions — not saying these will be your most effective options, but they will take up real estate.

Since this is all really detailed work, it will be very challenging. As you're aware, you really need to understand each role and all the details of that role to flush out the real requirements. The further you dig and more time you spend in this analysis, the better your results will be in the end. If finding the "gold nuggets" of information were easy, everybody would have already done this. To assist with this analysis, consider some of the following approaches to drive out the gold nuggets.

Approach for Identifying the "Gold Nuggets": Informational Interactions, Key Metrics, and KPI's.

A) The "5 Why" Method™

One sure way to get real requirements is to ask why many times. If you apply the 5 Why Method™, you will find the answer you're really looking for. For example:

User: I use this spreadsheet.
You: Why?
User: Because I need to see Expense information.
You: Why?
User: Because I need to compare expenses to Budget for the Management team.
You: Why?
User: Because we have monthly meetings where I am responsible to explain variances.
You: Why?
User: Because Department Managers are responsible for variances of 5 percent or more.
You: Why?
User: Because that's our job.

Ah ha.

We found a gold nugget! Department Managers need the following metric:
→ Monthly, Budget-to-Expense Variance, Variance %, and drill
to detail by Department

B) The Relationship

Focus on the relationship...like talking to a friend. Do not proceed to get requirements like you would in a traditional analysis session. You do not want to ask open-ended questions like "What do you need or want." This will not work. You really need to develop a relationship with each person to understand how they interact with their data. You need to sit down with them, gather information, and then return for more information. A good relationship will allow for better information exchange, better requirements, and more effective solution. If you do not develop a relationship, you will not find out the real requirements and metrics that that role has or that the person really needs.

Just to give you an indicator of a successful relationship, I'd consider using the Rule of 3™. From experience, the Rule of 3™ dictates that it will take you at least 3 sessions with a user to really get to the requirements you're looking for. That is where the magic really happens.

C) The Gold Nuggets

If you develop a relationship and proceed with the 5 Why approach, you will find yourself uncovering information that has never been seen. These informational requirements will be relative "gold nuggets" to the organization. These are key metrics that are used to make decisions. They are usually derived — never documented, never discussed, but regularly used in the decision-making process. In reality, these are the driving factors in the success or failure of that person and that department. You can be sure many of these "gold nuggets" can be traced to show some connection or impact to the company's bottom line.

<u>The Types of Gold Nuggets</u>
As you uncover and document the reporting metrics and KPI's that people use to do their jobs on a daily basis, you'll end up seeing a number of different types and variations. I've listed some examples below:

- **Types:** Basic Informational, Operational, Transactional, Alerts, Decisional

- **Level:** Aggregate, Summary, Detail

- **Time/Degrees Of Data:** Real-time, Almost Real-Time, Historical, Forecast/Prediction

- **Data Locations/Ownership:** Internal, External

- **User Location:** Desktop, Home, Device

- **Content Type:** Data (Intelligent, Dumb), Images, Sound, Video

3) Metrics and KPI's

Now with more understanding of the types of interactions and insight in how to find the gold nugget requirements, let's get back to our work. Step 1 and Step 2 prepared us to help document everything we need as inputs for this final step. Having requirements for reach role leads us to further define these elements and determine how and where they exist.

As we discussed at the end of FKM in Step 2, transactional and content management interactions are important to note and will allow for a completely integrated solution in the end. But, the real gold nuggets and the primary focus of our initial work will be uncovered in the areas of reporting, information, knowledge, and intelligence. These requirements often reveal themselves as some form of calculations using a base level of reporting metrics. So, for this next step, let's focus on the reporting side of metrics and KPI's.

<u>Analyzing and Locating Required Data/Information</u>
Once you have an understanding of the informational requirements for each role, the next logical step is to document the definitions of these Metrics and KPI's. Then we'll need to try and map these requirements to the existing

data architecture to see what exists and what does not. This is almost a traditional application development approach once you have the real requirements in front of you.

Tasks:
1) Document the definition/calculation for each Metric/KPI.
2) Document current storage location. (In current data architecture? Anywhere?)
3) Map the data element from source to destination.

As per this exercise, you'll find the data may exist in a wide variety of places. Here are some examples:
1) Internal
   a) Database (Oracle)
   b) PC (Excel)
   c) File System (Microsoft)
   d) Email
   e) Someone's Head
   f) Napkin in someone's pocket
2) External
   a) Data Vendors
   b) Data Providers
   c) Partners
   d) Internet
   e) Etc.

Following the tasks shown above in this exercise, you'll need to take the informational interactions and requirements you've uncovered and map them back to the data flow architecture and existing systems. As I mentioned, this is traditionally IT work, yet is still very important. Here's a worksheet example:

Metric/ Detail	Source Type	Source	Source Details	Destination
Hours worked	Database	PROD DB	Schema. Table Name	BI Report 1
Top Customer	Excel Spreadsheet	C:\	Susie PC	Mkt. Rpt.
Best Lead	Napkin	-	-	Scorecard
BI ROI %	Someone's head	-	-	Scorecard

Table 6.7

Once you've completed this exercise, you will have completed Stage I and will have a clear understanding of the group, department, or organization you chose to work with. Basically, you have all the requirements you need to move forward in planning the projects that will take your requirements and plan for the creation of the database, ETL, reporting, and related design and development for the Information Asset. So, now it's off to Stage II to identify the projects and create the Project Roadmap.

Stage II: Project Identification and Roadmap

4) Projects Identification and Roadmap

Once you have all the requirements for the Decision Intelligence Model™ from Stage I, then it's time to initiate bringing the Information Asset to life. You are now ready to begin planning the projects that will complete the actual development work to build all the required components of the solution. The projects can actually cover a wide range of activities, but will fall into the following primary categories:

1) Data Flow Architecture
2) Solution Delivery
3) Process and Support

Here are some examples of projects to capture in the roadmap.

Areas	Project
Solution Delivery	Reports for Partners.
	BI solution for Finance Dept
	Data Analysis cubes for Marketing.
	Analytics for Internal and External Customers.
Data Flow Architecture	Build XYZ data mart.
	Build Enterprise ETL Solution.
	Extend ODS functionality.
	Hardware upgrades.
	BI software tool installation.

Process and Support	Build QA environments.
	Model QA/Test and Release Process.
	Implement Report Request Process.

Table 6.8

Identifying projects and project planning is standard practice in every business today. There's nothing special in this exercise other than to make sure you've identified all the right projects for the right reasons. Project planning and implementation will drive the work to meet the vision. The Roadmap will be the strategy and plan to ensure integration and consistency. Since we reviewed the Data Flow Architecture for required improvements and gathered very detailed requirements for the Decision Intelligence Model™, we know we're ready. From our perspective, we can be sure that:

1) We understand where we're going first with the Information Asset.

2) We're planning for the right projects to get us there.

These are the core objectives of the Information Asset — Project Roadmap. The Roadmap deliverable will be the High-Level and Detailed-Level project planning documentation. So put on your project planner hat or call the PMO, because Stage II is all about project planning. You can do this work in whatever tool you use for these activities. Microsoft Project is a popular choice. After this planning exercise is done, we're on our way to creation.

Stage III: Working On The Projects To Build The Information Asset™

Stage III is all about creation and implementation. If we've done quality work up to this point, we're now sure we're heading in the right direction. The three major areas of project work are that can be addressed in parallel will be:

1) Data Flow Architecture
2) Solution Delivery
3) Process and Support

5) Data Flow Architecture

As we discussed in substantial detail in Chapter IV, the data flow architecture is a critical foundation component of the Information Asset. Many projects will need to occur in this component of the Information Asset to ensure a successful final solution.

6) Solution Delivery

The second key project area is the end product of a great data flow architecture. It's about the solutions that consistently deliver the data, information, knowledge, and intelligence to the user community. The projects in this area are solely focused on the users. Here are some objectives in this area:

1) Addressing new business needs through the Information Asset.
2) Learning new features and techniques to enhance reporting capabilities.
3) Creating a Knowledge Management Department or BI Competency Center to support solutions.
4) Adding new content and features or functionality to the solutions.
5) Managing and adapting to changes.
6) Communication, awareness, and training extended into user communities.

7) Process and Support

These are primarily the people and process projects that will need to take place to support the solution.

Some examples of process efforts include:
1) Dev — QA — Prod
2) Production Release
3) Requests Processes
   a) Assistance

b) Projects
4) Support

On the people side of the equation, there will be a lot of work to do as well. Here are some examples:

1) Staffing
2) Organizational Changes
3) Assignments and Resource Allocation
4) Skills
5) Training

Usually, on many technology projects, these are the efforts that get swept to the side because of time or money constraints. Since we are planning to build a successful Information Asset that will stand the test of time, people and process-related projects need to be addressed all along the way.

Challenges

Now that we've covered all of the steps in "The Recipe," let's see what challenges we might face along the way. By far the most challenging and difficult aspect of accomplishing the "Information Asset" will be successfully dealing with the following issues. You will encounter all of these along the way, and without a "thick skin," you may lose track of or be diverted from your goal and objectives.

- **Data Ownership/Territory** — Many organizations have employees or departments who either pride themselves in building their own little IT departments or proceed to do so out of necessity. Many times a slow, red-tape-plagued or unresponsive technology department feeds this fire in the short-term and cause long-term issues. In either case, these information pockets cause a substantial amount of fragmentation, issues in the data flow, and corresponding priority problems when trying to establish a corporate-wide architecture solution.

- **Information Autocracies** — Information is power, and people who crave power know this. Some people will do everything they can to stop the knowledge sharing or the documentation of their roles. They think the information they use to make decisions is special and don't realize that the information belongs to the organization. Everyone is replaceable. Every company should be prepared to provide all people with the information they need and a method to fill in the blanks.

- **Politics** — You'll never be able to get away from politics, and this type of project is not an exception. There will be many attempts to change, alter, and add to the agenda of the effort all along the way by many people.

- **Organizational Priorities** — Obviously, every organization has different priorities at different times in its history. Building the Information Asset can be done at all stages of the growth of a company, but making sure the project is a top priority is major benefit.

- **Timing** — Timing is always important. You would not want to start this project as a company is failing in its core business and looking to close its doors or sell. Making this investment would be appropriate as part of a growth or maintenance strategy.

- **Security** — I've noticed this topic get hotter by the year, and the reality is that the Information Asset has many benefits to properly support building and maintaining an appropriate corporate security model.

- **Power Struggle** — Unfortunately, this project will drive out power struggles between people. When you see irrational and uncooperative behavior, you're seeing this in practice.

- **Tech/Business Skills**
  - o How users identify their needs? — This is rarely done in businesses today don't expect much when you start your work.

  - o How IT gathers requirements? — Once again, not many IT people have the expertise needed to ask the right questions and design the appropriate solutions.

  - o How IT builds and manages solutions? — This is a very important concern that will need to be addressed along the way.

- **All Existing Efforts** — There are probably many efforts underway to try to piece together solutions that are parts of the Information Asset. These efforts are problems initially because of overlap. If you manage this correctly, these could be transformed into logical extensions of the Information Asset effort.

- **Change** — You will feel the resistance. You will live the pain.

- **Organizational Boundaries** — Different management, different opinions, and different direction always help confuse project teams. The best case for your work is that everyone is aligned under some umbrella of Knowledge Management, BI Competency Center, or even just the Information Asset Team.

- **Current Focus** — Staffing technology "firefighters" has become more the direction of technology departments in recent years rather than staffing for strategic value. Just getting and keeping people who can KTLO ("Keep The Lights On") may be the current focus, but the mindset will need to change with Information Asset capable resources.

So with these challenges in mind, the next question is "Why are these things happening?" Or, "What has caused some of the challenges?" In some cases, it's circumstance, human nature, or even specific area-related issues. Listed below are examples of some contributing mindsets that drive the challenges we face:

- **View of Reporting** — Until recently with business intelligence, reporting has always been the "redheaded step-child" of application development. Left without attention and focus, industrious resources have made this their charge — to find, assemble, and deliver information with their favorite desktop tool.

- **Data Fragmentation** — You can blame this on the client-server era. You can blame Microsoft Access and Excel for being so easy to learn and use. You can blame quick-and-dirty solutions being easier to throw together than it is to work with the IT departments. The bottom line is that most organizations have data and information everywhere. This is standard and consistent problem that data analysis or business intelligence drives out into the open.

- **Role-based Information Autocracies** — If they can't get it from somewhere else, they'll build it, own it, and hide it from mostly everyone else.

- **"Politics"** — The root of many evils strikes again. Let's say it's not doing the right thing, but doing the thing that is in the best interest of that particular person.

- **Training and Skills in BI** — Sorry, but very few people "get it" when it comes to business intelligence concepts today. It takes desire and time to learn these skills.

- **Silver Bullet Syndrome** — You've seen this from every weak-minded middle manager on the payroll: Buy a software product to solve your problems. Nice try. Never works. A BI tool will never make your "almost-a-data-model" tables join correctly or make your bad data correct and valid.

- **Bending the Line** — Another one of my favorites. Middle management just keeps adjusting project direction until the solution solves less and less, and then just ends up looking like the same problem you tried to solve. This technique is a method for management to pretend they're driving for change, but to really drive against it informally.

- **Focus on Software, Not Solutions** — Another noise-making distraction — blaming software products instead of poor solution development.

Preparing for the Challenges

Making an attempt to work on the Information Asset will drive you directly into many of the issues I mentioned. To ensure you success, make note of the following requirements or support systems to help you on your way:

1) **Organizational Sponsorship** — The Recipe for the Informational Asset absolutely requires the organization to support the efforts financially and emotionally. The work will be difficult enough on its own.

2) **Direct Management Support** — You also must have direct management support or the support of someone with authority over the highest level of the organization you're working in. Once again, without this you'd be in a real tough spot.

3) **Talented, Experienced, and Knowledgeable Technical and Business Team Members** — I believe this is an absolute requirement as well. Weaker team members often require a lot of time and attention and take away from the projects. The quality of the solution will be a direct reflection of the quality and ability of every team member and the leadership of team management.

4) **3 P's: Projects, Pay, People** — I always discuss these three requirements I have for any project,

105

work, or position I may chose to take. In my experience, these are the qualifying reasons people take jobs and stay at jobs. If you're very happy with all three, you never leave the job. If you're really happy with two of the three, you hang in there. If you're only happy with one or less, you are looking to leave for sure. The Information Asset will require investment in all three categories for staffing, but will pay off in the long run.

Summary

With all we've discussed with the Recipe for Building the Information Asset, I'm sure you can see the value and recognize the challenges. We're not talking about preparing a fast-food meal here, but rather a gourmet organic feast fit for a king. Only the finest ingredients will do, and the result will be worth it.

Chapter VII

<u>Ensuring Your Legacy</u>

**"You only heard the world was flat.
What's stopping you from sailing
over the horizon to find out?"**

Chapter VII – Ensuring Your Legacy

"You only heard the world was flat. What's stopping you from sailing over the horizon to find out?"

Alright, we have heard it all before: "I don't have the budget to do this." "I don't have the resources to do this." "I don't have buy-in from the business." Well, I think that at many points throughout history, people say things like that about all new inventions and opportunities. From never being able to sail around the world, to never being able to fly, to never reaching the moon — there have always been and will always be valid reasons something can't be done. But who's to say you can't be the person who starts the new trend? Without real innovation and progress, we'd all still be walking around with candles, dreaming of indoor plumbing, and tending to our horses. Since the light bulb, toilets, and cars are already standards in our lives, why not be the person who invents and delivers something truly revolutionary in business in relation to information systems and reporting? Over time, it seems that somehow good technologies and solutions always find their way past the naysayers and make it to general acceptance. I know there's a future magazine cover with your name and picture on it if you find ways to realize this potential.

The responsibility of creating a legacy through a career falls directly on the shoulders of each individual. The basic business challenges are out there along with the unique effort-specific challenges we've discussed along the way. The question is, are you willing to proceed? In all we've discussed, there are many opportunities to take the Crawl/Walk/Run approach as long as you know where you're going. There are many Data Flow Architecture projects to get done. There are many Decision Intelligence requirements and design projects to complete. And, finally, there's combining each of these into a consistent Solution Delivery and Management system. If you're committed to any of this, perhaps you really only need a little follow-through to create the legacy.

Let's just consider this similar to the follow-through on your basketball shot or golf swing. It's the icing on the cake. Once you've created the organizational blueprint with the Decision Intelligence Model™ and delivered The Information Asset™

with a strong Data Flow Architecture and Intelligent Reporting Solution, then the easy part will be ensuring your legacy. We've already set the vision in this book. Find any way to make it happen and you can get there. With the understanding that it may take years for you to reach this goal, here are some guidelines to use along the way.

Measuring Success

You can measure success and progress along the way by generating your own set of metrics that can be used as Key Performance Indicators for the Information Asset itself. Some example metrics are shown below:

- ### Data Flow Architecture

Metric/KPI	Current	Expected
Amount of data elements in data warehouse	30%	100%
End-To-End Data Flow	20%	100%
ETL Outages	12/mth	1 per yr
Data Quality (1 to 10, with 10 as best)	2	10
Number of Reporting Platforms	18	1

- ### Solution Delivery

Metric/KPI	Current	Expected
Portal on every desktop	3%	100%
Number of Depts. using BI Competency Ctr.	52%	100%
Intelligent Reporting with Analytics	1%	80%

- ### Process and Support

Metric/KPI	Current	Expected
QA Defects Found	35/mth	1/mth
Reporting requests using KM Dept.	10%	90%
BI Competency Center FTE's	0	12

By creating and managing to Metrics and KPI's as shown above, you'll be able to begin to really measure the success of your progress.

Maintenance

Another key concern to address along the way would be the maintenance of the existing solutions along with the new development and direction. As with any new solution, even one as important as this, you will still need constant maintenance and continuous improvement of all components as the shift to the Information Asset is occurring.

The business world will not stand still, so, as always, it's important to continue to oil the machine and sharpen the saw. Since every business today needs to focus on this type of work already, it is almost standard practice to include maintenance into all planning. My only advice here would be to make sure the right people are in place with the right mindset to resolve issues as they arise. As simple as this sounds, a good maintenance team always helps keep key resources focused on the new direction and the consistent quality of the new solutions.

Horizons: Integrating with the Future

Building for today is one thing, but keeping current with what the future holds is a completely separate focus. Just like you'll see many companies dominating one part of technology history, they usually find themselves playing catch-up or are gone in the next. Web 2.0, digital content, blogging, search, unstructured content, and mobile devices of many types and purposes continue to drive innovation and new business system applications.

It's always interesting to see what the future holds and how businesses absorb and adapt to new technology. Remember life in Corporate America before email? Before the Internet? Remember life in general before cell phones? These advances in technology are all subcomponents of the Information Asset. New communication methods, content creators, content storage applications, development and delivery platforms, sales channels, etc. — the list goes on and on, but the innovation and change remains constant.

No one knows what the future holds, but I guarantee you that data, information, knowledge, and intelligence will continue be a very important part of it. Keep up on new trends and invite new innovations to continue to transform the Information Asset in your organization. Allowing for change will allow for growth, help ensure your legacy today, and secure that legacy for years to come.

Conclusion

Every business has assets. For years, a critical and very valuable organizational asset has gone unnoticed and has been taken for granted. This asset is The Information Asset™. The Information Asset™ is the circulatory and nervous system of the organization. There are three primary components of The Information Asset™, which include the Data Flow Architecture, Decision Intelligence Model™, and Solutions Delivery and Management. Many of the pieces that make up these components already exist in organizations today, but no one has been able to put all the pieces together. There is a huge opportunity to collect, store, transform, and present information and knowledge to users to increase the effectiveness of decision-making. Instead of focusing on technology as a cost or expense, organizations really need to understand the value of the systems within. The information systems that have been assembled with fantastic technology over the past thirty-plus years can enable and empower the future of every company.

The Information Asset is a pure blueprint of how an organization works and operates. The roles people have, the informational interactions, the Metrics/KPI's, and the decisions are all important assets that need to be recognized and utilized for future value and success. There is no good reason that every employee should not have access to all the data, information, knowledge, and intelligence he or she will need on the day they start their new job. There should be a portal on every desktop with the information interactions and links to the details people need. There is no good reason executives and upper management of organizations need to keep flying blind while trying to compete in the marketplace and make their company as successful as possible. People have been using dashboards in cars and planes for years to provide Metrics and KPI's to operate this machinery. Why would management be any different? The technology exists, and the Information Asset is the solution that brings it all together.

Do you remember the scenario/example I used in the Introduction? Well, let's just fast forward a few years in that example. The scene is still a large boardroom. Managers have just arrived from across the organization for a very important meeting. Today our company will decide [something really important, once again]. The information and intelligence used to make this decision needs to be accurate and up-to-the-minute. Fortunately, the company just completed building a strong, scalable, and powerful infrastructure known as The Information Asset™. The managers have arrived with current, accurate, and consistent decision intelligence.

The financial, HR, marketing, and sales information has all come from the same information system. Everyone trusts the information they have and information others have. The conversation is now only focused on making the right decision. The executives have predictive capabilities, analytics, and historical trends. It's amazing how different this situation is and how effective this company now can be in running the business. With all of this, the meeting starts…

As the discussion ensues, it becomes apparent that this management team is as ready as it has ever been to make decisions through the use of business and decision intelligence. There is no more arguing and guessing. There are no fear or power struggles over who has valid information and who has out-of-date information. There are just decisions being made based on valid and effective information, knowledge, and intelligence. The vehicle for this successful approach is the Information Asset™. Uncovering and organizing around this valuable and historically hidden organizational asset is absolutely the key to this success. Remember, every tomorrow will look like today unless we take steps to enable and enact effective change.

To the first movers in this space, there's a huge competitive advantage in working on the Information Asset. Since each organization and departments are at differing maturity levels, it's important to know where your organization or department is before you start. But no matter where you start from, this a unique point in technology history when you have this opportunity to make a big and lasting impact with the Information Asset. Can you? Will you? Are you a leader, or just a passenger on the bus? I don't know, because I don't know you directly. In any case, one thing I do know is that if you've stayed with me through this whole journey, I know you've been informed. What you do with this information, knowledge, and intelligence is up to you. Ready to leave a legacy?

Every tomorrow will look like today unless we take steps to enable and enact effective change. Only through quality work today can we build a better tomorrow.

$\mathbb{K}$